Poverty Amid Affluence

Oscar Ornati

Poverty Amid Affluence

A Report on a Research Project carried out

at the New School for Social Research

Prepared with the Editorial Assistance of **J. Stouder Sweet**

THE TWENTIETH

CENTURY FUND

NEW YORK · 1966

First published April 1966
Second printing August 1966

Copyright © 1966 by the Twentieth Century Fund, Inc.
Manufactured in the United States of America
Library of Congress Catalog Card Number: 66–18565

Foreword

In 1960 the Twentieth Century Fund became interested in the way pockets of poverty persisted even in an affluent society and seemed largely unaffected by the general rise in living standards. At about the same time, representatives of the New School for Social Research in New York came to us with a proposal for studies in this area.

The trustees of the Twentieth Century Fund decided to support these studies and researches. At that time Henry David, soon to become president of the New School, joined with Dr. Oscar Ornati, Professor of Economics in the Graduate School of the New School, in taking responsibility for this work. In the course of time changes took place, and Dr. Ornati has, during the last several years, carried forward the project on his own. His own interests, meanwhile, have led him to join temporarily the staff of the Office of Economic Opportunity.

On the following pages Dr. Ornati acknowledges the help that he has received from colleagues and associates along the way.

This small book represents, in effect, Dr. Ornati's report to the director and trustees of the Twentieth Century Fund on the substance and major findings of the New School research project. It has seemed to us of sufficient value to make it available to a larger audience. We thank Dr. Ornati for his long-continued concern for this project.

August Heckscher, Director
The Twentieth Century Fund

41 East 70th Street, New York
January 1966

v

Preface

The publication of John Kenneth Galbraith's The Affluent Society trig-
gered this study. Some of us at the New School for Social Research
felt that the time had come to break the link, traditional in economic
research, between the poverty of individuals and the poverty of nations: poverty must also be studied in the context of an affluent society. Following a brief statistical survey to establish a gross count
of the poor, plans for such a study were developed with Henry David,
then Dean of the Graduate Faculty of the New School. The Twentieth
Century Fund, which had been thinking along somewhat parallel lines,
agreed to sponsor the project and provided the money to carry it out.

Since the inception of this study, a coincidence of political and
intellectual events in the United States has propelled concern with poverty into a national commitment. Uneasiness about the displacement
of workers by automation, the new visibility of the school drop-out
problem and the civil rights protests have led to a plethora of speeches,
articles, pamphlets and books and, recently, to legislation and action.
Our research was thus carried out in a period when new considera-
tions, new ideas and new data were continually forcing themselves upon our attention.

Amid this flood of new thinking, it is particularly difficult to distinguish the direct from the indirect contributions to this study. We
sought out the ideas of all those who were beginning to be concerned
about poverty in the United States. To identify the perception of a
particular individual and to acknowledge it as the germ of an hypothesis or even a chapter is impossible. My first acknowledgement
thus must, in honesty and I hope with scientific detachment and precision, go to the times, the people and the country. For the rest I
can only describe the way the staff of the project worked and report on
how the various research topics were distributed among the staff
members.

Jointly with the staff of the Twentieth Century Fund, Henry David
and I decided to cast our work as much as possible in an institutional
framework. We tried to involve both faculty and students of the New
School in various aspects of the study. Consequently the study on
poverty led—directly and indirectly—to numerous lectures and courses
on related topics, to the completion of at least two doctoral disserta-
tions and the publication of several articles and, soon, books. In 1961,
in view of her work in consumption economics, Dr. Ruth Mack was
asked to join us to lecture on this topic and to help guide the study.

She was able to remain with us during the first year of the work. The plan of the Study was elaborated, without major changes, by the three of us in consultation with Isador Lubin of the Twentieth Century Fund. A number of graduate students were added to complete the staff.

The modus operandi that we adopted was to assign a broad topic to an individual who would survey the literature and collect the data, after which the project staff would discuss the findings and the problems encountered. This procedure resulted in staff papers on sixteen separate topics.

Sheila W. Bankhead with Dr. Mack's particular counsel was responsible for the collection of the many and varied budgets prepared through the years by public and private agencies, the construction of the "men's low-wage index" and the delineation of a poverty band. The notion of the "poverty band" and the emphasis given to it in this study resulted from the data's resistance to fit a preconceived line. This also emphasizes the crucial importance of differences between individual and social perceptions of poverty.

At the same time, Alfons Joachimowski (now teaching economics at the University of Saskatchewan) surveyed the history of economic thought on poverty and the more recent technical work on income distribution which helped shape the definition of poverty. Raymond G. Brown (then a candidate for the Ph. D. in economics and now a lecturer at Sarah Lawrence College) worked on the statistics of the incidence of poverty and its composition. From this information we developed the notion of "poverty-linked characteristics" and, with an assist from Professor John Van Lear, the Pi coefficient as the measure of the risk of poverty. Mr. Brown was assisted in his work by Mrs. Helen Ginsburg. Mrs. Ginsburg (who is at present teaching economics at Queensborough Community College, in New York) worked at length on the housing condition of the poor and on relief expenditures data which were used in the calculation of the anti-poverty dollar. The psychological aspects of the health problems of the poor were studied by Mrs. Phyllis Myers, while Mr. Joachimowski dealt with the problems of physical health and the cost of care. Mrs. Myers also worked on the problems of the education of the poor and on a survey of the literature of "dropping-out." Professor Adolf Lowe served admirably as moderator and as critic of the make-up of the anti-poverty dollar. Mrs. Bankhead worked valiantly in extricating the data that comprise that total and deserves particular credit for separating out the administrative costs.

Mrs. Voltarine Garst was our administrative officer. She also contributed to the analysis of income of women heads of households, to the study of infant mortality by income class, and to the analysis of income distribution of the group we labeled "non-white, non-Negro." In addition Mrs. Garst helped Alyce Slossberg in typing the manuscript, and worked on a variety of other topics connected with unemployment and minimum wages.

The Twentieth Century Fund not only made the study possible, but helped by bringing together a consulting committee that read the interim papers and met to hear progress reports. The members of this committee—Arthur F. Burns, Wilbur Cohen, Robert Lampman, Adolf Lowe, Isador Lubin, Eleanor Snyder, John Van Laer and Arthur Vidich—gave graciously of their time and knowledge. Throughout, the staff of the Twentieth Century Fund and members of the faculty of the New School gave guidance and support. Thomas R. Carskadon and Mrs. Elizabeth Blackert, of the Fund, deserve particular thanks for their patience, while Felicia Deyrup, David Schwartzam and Saul Padover must be mentioned among those from the New School. J. Stouder Sweet ably assisted with the final editing and shaping of the report.

Despite the many contributions, all of which are gratefully acknowledged, the final responsibility for the report summarized here is, nevertheless, mine.

Work in the field of poverty has just begun. My concern, and I hope the nation's, will continue. In staying with it, I have been helped by W. E. B. O., who insisted that the problem of poverty was too serious to be left to an economist and that whatever was said had to accord with political and psychological reality as well as with common sense.

                                                          Oscar Ornati

Washington, D. C., January 1966

Contents

PART THREE

LIST OF TABLES

LIST OF CHARTS

"Although the economic well-being and prosperity of the United States have progressed to a level surpassing any achieved in world history, and although these benefits are widely shared throughout the Nation, poverty continues to be the lot of a substantial number of our people.

"The United States can achieve its full economic and social potential as a nation only if every individual has the opportunity to contribute to the full extent of his capabilities and to participate in the workings of our society.

"It is, therefore, the policy of the United States to eliminate the paradox of poverty in the midst of plenty in this Nation by opening to everyone the opportunity for education and training, the opportunity to work, and the opportunity to live in decency and dignity."

Economic Opportunity Act of 1964,
Public Law 88-452, August 20, 1964

Introduction

WE AS A nation have been concerned with poverty. At least, we speak and write more about the poor than any other civilized country does.

Since 1900 American concern with poverty has distinguished between the poor and "paupers." "Paupers" were those who had given up the struggle, who could not be reclaimed.[1] The poor worked hard, had self-respect, cherished their independence. Everyday circumstances over which they had no control pushed the "worthy poor" into "pauperism." From about 1900 to 1932, the fight against poverty was seen in terms of laws regarding tenement housing, abolition of child labor, maximum hours, minimum wages, and compensation for industrial accidents. The problems of environment were recognized, those of adjusting the individual to it and it to the individual were not. After the New Deal the distinction between the poor and "paupers" disappeared and poverty was viewed increasingly as a matter of economics. The poor became thought of as the product of the economy working at less than full potential, and poverty as a drag on the forward march of the economy. This notion found expression in the Employment Act of 1946. After World War II, the United States moved into affluence. But poverty did not go away. With the passage of the Economic Opportunity Act in 1964 it became a major concern of the government.

Today, while much is being done, and while new data and insights on how to do away with poverty are becoming available, there is still little consensus as to what poverty is, as to the size of the problem, the actions to be taken to do away with it, or the dangers to our society of not doing away with it. There is no consistent theoretical explanation of poverty within the framework of any social discipline. And this study provides none.

Poverty is variously defined as being "subjective," "objective," or "relative." It is viewed as involving "insufficiency" or "inequality" or both.

Subjective poverty refers to the individual's "feeling" rich or poor, according to the range of currently available goods and services he might reasonably expect to enjoy. Nobody, for instance, felt poor a hundred years ago who did not have electric light. Today it is taken for granted that even poor people in the United States should have electric light. It is an accepted part of the U. S. style of life at even the

---

1. See Robert H. Bremner, Change and Continuity in Recent American Concepts of Poverty, paper presented October 25, 1962, Faculty Seminar on Urban Poverty, Hunter College, The City University of New York, pp. 3 and 4.

lowest level. Although electric light is not absolutely necessary to life, we feel deprived without it. Subjective poverty is also determined by a myriad of other psychological and sociological forces which have been analyzed in writings on social stratification and social status, and on status-seeking and life in the suburbs. The poverty study staff of the New School for Social Research, while aware of the problems of subjective poverty, has not concerned itself with it as such. Similarly we have not concerned ourselves with the so-called "voluntary" poverty of the recluse, the beatnik, the mendicant orders, and the ascetic. Our concern is with "objective" poverty—involuntary poverty, as defined by U. S. society in the twentieth century.

Poverty is often treated as a matter of inequality. From this viewpoint, one can say that the poor are always with us. If the poor are defined as making up some part of the bottom of the income distribution, some kind of lower fifth, eighth, tenth, or whatever fraction might be chosen, their eternal permanence is guaranteed. This approach creates poverty by definition. It is not that policy concern with income distribution is unimportant, but rather that income distribution is to be accepted for what it is—a derivative aspect of poverty rather than, so to speak, its definitional cause. While not unmindful of the problems of income distribution, the New School study staff has primarily focused its attention on the poverty of insufficiency rather than on the poverty of inequality.

In terms of insufficiency, poverty has traditionally been considered to be the condition of persons whose resources have been insufficient to satisfy minimum needs. The resources with which we have concerned ourselves have been the individuals' incomes—savings have been found to be almost insignificant for this group. In the determination of minimum needs, he who is "poor" is found traditionally to be the individual living below "minimum subsistence," the individual whose essential needs are not being "adequately" met, who lives in "deprivation." Having agreed that nobody should live below "subsistence" or be "deprived," we seem, as a nation, unable to agree as to exactly what we mean. Even the physical sciences are of small help in determining "minimum needs." One component of need, "adequate nutrition," for instance, is not scientifically definable. Among nutrition experts, estimated protein requirements are little more than intelligent guesswork; there is doubt about desirable intakes of calcium, iron, and vitamins. As one student of the subject has noted, "the problem is rather like that of trying to define 'adequate' individual height."[1]

1. Peter Townsend, "The Meaning of Poverty," British Journal of Sociology, September 1962, p. 220.

People differ with respect to their ideas of what constitutes need, their feeling of justice, their values. Their estimates of need will differ according to whether they are themselves poor or not poor, thrifty or lax, interested in things or ideas, conversant with or ignorant of the lives of the poor. Their explicit and implicit notions about the workings of the economy and the society become crucially important. They will view levels of poverty as unacceptable depending on whether they are by training economists, sociologists, or engineers; possibly on whether they were trained at Harvard or Chicago; whether or not "survival of the fittest" sums up their social outlook.

The New School study, surveying efforts to define poverty, describes a changing climate of opinion. It finds a shifting content of various styles of life designated by social workers and public administrators as "subsistence," "adequacy," and "minimum comfort." These are American styles of life, as Americans themselves have seen them.

PART ONE

The poverty band

POVERTY in this study is defined as the lack of command over goods and services sufficient to meet minimum needs.

Objectively, poverty can be measured in terms of the proportion of currently agreed-upon basic "necessities" that income can buy. Most necessary to human health and well-being, everybody will agree, are basic food, shelter, and clothing. Those who measure poverty quantitatively will concentrate their attention on these necessities. Those concerned with more than bare subsistence will ask another question—are all Americans sharing reasonably well in the current U. S. affluence? Such critics will be interested in income inequality as well as in insufficiency. In addition to lacking the barest necessities of life, being "poor" in the United States in the 1960's may also mean that one belongs to the bottom 20 per cent of the population that receives less than 5 per cent of total family personal income. One can be poor, then, from an insufficiency of food, clothing, and housing. Or one can be poor from having a much less than proportionate share in available goods and services.

Standards of Sufficiency

Most writers on poverty have used a single poverty "line." Sometimes they have made comparisons between one period and another in terms of a static, unchanging line. Obviously, investigators using different "lines" will differ in their assessment of the extent of poverty at any particular time.

The "poverty line" concept was popularized by Charles Booth, an English sociologist, in his Life and Labour of the People in London (17 vols., London, 1891-1903). Booth divided the people of London into eight income groups. The bottom four groups he described as "living below the line of poverty." He estimated that 30 per cent of the population of London lived below the "poverty line." These were described as living "under a struggle to obtain the necessaries of life and make

both ends meet" or "living in a state of chronic want." Booth defined
those who lived at or below the "poverty line" as "having at most an income which at one time with another averages 21 shillings or 22 shillings per week for a very small family (or up to 25 or 26s. for one of a
larger size), and in many cases falling much below this level."

In 1899, B. Seebohm Rowntree, another British investigator,
carried the "line" concept further, and assigned weekly minimum monetary allowances for food, housing, clothing, light, fuel, and other necessities for adults and children. No allowance was made for any expenditure on moral, mental, or social development, for transportation,
or even for postage stamps. This budgetary standard Rowntree defined
as the "primary poverty line." Having established this standard, he
tried to ascertain what proportion of the population of York, England,
a town of 76,000 in 1899, were then living at or below the line of "primary poverty." Rowntree also attempted to measure the number of
those living below what he termed the "secondary poverty line." Secondary poverty assumed some injudicious spending. Both lines judged
the available family income insufficient to maintain "physical efficiency." Rowntree found that 10 per cent of the population of York were
living in "primary poverty"—a level at which even families of exem-
plary prudence could not maintain health and efficiency. Eighteen per
cent were living in "secondary poverty"; a total of 28 per cent were
living in poverty of one or the other kind.[1]

The path first charted by Booth and Rowntree that called for the
setting of standards of sufficiency by way of minimum budgets has been
followed by many others in the United States as well as in the rest of
the world. Most U.S. budgets, since the earliest quantity budgets in
the early 1900's, were prepared for purposes other than time comparisons—to determine eligibility for private charity or public relief benefits or services, to establish a minimum "fair" wage for workers involved in labor disputes, or to establish an "American standard of
living." In each case, U.S. budget-makers were interested in establishing living standards valid for a particular time only. But they followed Rowntree's procedure of drawing up a quantity budget, one that
specified how much might be spent on food, clothing, and other items,
and sometimes went into details of living space, calorie intake per
person, and so on.

In recent years, U.S. writers on poverty have utilized several of
the best known among these budgets as the starting point in defining
their own "poverty line." For instance, both Robert J. Lampman, in

1. B. Seebohm Rowntree, Poverty: A Study of Town Life, Longmans, Green
and Co., London, 1901, 1922.

a study prepared in 1959 for the Joint Economic Committee of the U.S.
Congress, and Gabriel Kolko in a 1962 study of Wealth and Power in
America used the Bureau of Labor Statistics' City Worker's Family
Budget (1947) as their initial point of reference. [1] The Conference on
Economic Progress in a 1960 report on poverty and deprivation used
the Bureau's later, more generous Interim City Worker's Family Budget (1959). In 1962, James N. Morgan and associates of the University
of Michigan Survey Research Center in a report on U.S. income and
welfare used a family budget published in 1959 by the Community Council of Greater New York. [2] While all four studies went to actual administrative definitions for help in defining poverty, they themselves
adopted arbitrary "lines." These lines represented a compromise between the comfort and subsistence extremes.

Kolko (who adjusted the 1947 BLS City Worker's Family Budget
for price change, with an additional 1.8 per cent thrown in for good
measure) used $4,500 for a "maintenance level of living" in 1959 and
70 per cent of that, or $3,150, for an "emergency" level of living.
Lampman used a cut-off of $2,516 for a four-person family, a figure
described as "well below the $4,000 which the Bureau of Labor Statis-
tics has estimated is necessary for an urban family of four to maintain
an 'adequate standard of living,'" but "well above the budget levels
used in determining need in public assistance programs in most states."

The Conference on Economic Progress report and the Michigan
study apply an income concept which includes some items of non-money
income. The Michigan findings are based on a sample survey. They
use gross disposable income, which includes imputed rent and excludes
federal income tax liability. The estimate of need is based on the budget of the Community Council of Greater New York, and the adjustment
for differing needs was most sophisticated. This budget posits $4,330
for a family of four. The Michigan staff worked out a budget for each
type of family surveyed, based not only on family size but also on employment status. Further, a family was considered poor only if the

1. Both Lampman and Kolko used the Current Population Reports series on
income distribution and made family size adjustment after the method of Dorothy
Brady (and Kellogg) in "City Workers' Family Budgets," Bureau of Labor Statistics Bulletin 927, March 1948.

2. Robert J. Lampman, The Low Income Population and Economic Growth,
Study Paper No. 12, Joint Economic Committee, 86th Cong., 1st sess., 1959;
Gabriel Kolko, Wealth and Power in America, Praeger, New York, 1962; Pov-
erty and Deprivation in the United States, Conference on Economic Progress,
Washington, 1962; James N. Morgan, Martin H. David, Wilbur J. Cohen, and
Harvey E. Brazer, Income and Welfare in the United States, Survey Research
Center, University of Michigan, McGraw-Hill, New York, 1962.

gross disposable income unit fell below 90 per cent of the calculated
budget needs <u>and</u> the family had less than $5,000 in savings.[1]

The Conference on Economic Progress used the same Office of
Business Economics personal income distribution series as the Michigan study. "Needs" were put at $4,000 for a family of any size, and
$2,000 for an individual. These levels are adaptations from the 1959
BLS Interim City Worker's Family Budget, which details a considerably higher level of living than the 1947 BLS budget used by Kolko.
Poverty, here, is defined as income below two-thirds the median cost
of the 1959 Interim City Worker's Family Budget as priced in twenty
cities. Families were considered to be living above poverty, but in
"deprivation," if living on an income between $4,000 and $6,000; for
unattached individuals the corresponding figures were between $2,000
and $3,000. Thus deprivation was defined as being family income less
than the $6,000 City Worker's Family Budget median and more than the
$4,000 poverty cut-off. The authors felt that the level represented by
the actual budget reflects, in a sense, "the borderline between deprivation and real comfort." Although no explicit family-size adjustments
were made in the Conference on Economic Progress study, the choice
of appropriate income levels involved implicit adjustments. For instance, the $4,000 level was chosen to make allowance for regional
variation in living costs and after examination of the relationship between family size and income.

As Rowntree had done, Kolko and the Conference on Economic
Progress tacitly recognized the existence of the poverty continuum by
defining two separate poverty levels ("emergency" and "maintenance"
in Kolko; "poverty" and "deprivation" in the report of the Conference
on Economic Progress). Neither Kolko nor the Conference, however,
recognized the full width of the "spread" or "band" that results when
all contemporary, operational definitions of poverty are plotted on a
chart. Neither described poverty in terms of the lower relief budgets
prevailing in many states today. Nor did Lampman or Morgan.

Taking a different approach, the staff of the New School poverty
study developed a three-level "band" concept to synthesize definitions
of poverty in the United States in the twentieth century. The sources
used were some sixty budgets for workers' families prepared over the
years by governmental and private agencies. A list of such budgets is
given in Appendix 1. These budgets are operational definitions of poverty, for various administrative purposes such as the payment of money

---

1. The study found, however, that for families with "inadequate" incomes
"the average amount of savings used in 1959 was about $150." Michigan, op. cit.,
p. 190.

for relief. They provide a reliable index of contemporary practice and a rough social consensus about who is "poor." Starting from such budgets, it is possible, as we show in Appendix 2, to arrive at the dollar amounts required, year by year, to maintain a four-member family, consisting of an employed father, an unemployed mother, and two minor children, at levels of "minimum subsistence," "minimum adequacy," and "minimum comfort." The accompanying chart (Figure 1) portrays the three-level "poverty band" so constructed for the years 1905 to 1960.

The titles "minimum subsistence," "minimum adequacy," and "minimum comfort" have actually been applied to some of the budgets by their makers. One or another can be used to categorize all of them. These different definitions reflect differences in what society intends to do about individuals and families lacking the income described as necessary for certain minimum packages of goods and services—grant relief payments, for instance, or authorize individuals to receive the services of social welfare agencies, or bring them under minimum-wage legislation. By standards commonly used today by state agencies dispensing Aid to Dependent Children and relief funds, four-member urban families that fall below the "subsistence" line used in this study are considered eligible for relief. This level of need is tied closely to food, clothing, and shelter, plus a few other needs, such as carfare to work or to seek work. The second level, called "minimum adequacy," is today usually used to determine whether or not a family is eligible for welfare agency services other than direct money payments. The "adequacy" level is approximately a median between the "subsistence" and "minimum comfort" levels. The top level, "minimum comfort," represents the threshold of "comfort," as comfort is viewed in contemporary terms. This level represents the minimum once considered necessary for "health and decency" for civil service and other workers.

Circularity in Criteria for Budgets

Budget-makers customarily base their budgets on (1) what people "ought" to buy and (2) what they actually do buy. In establishing the food component of the budget, for instance, they estimate what minimum diet an adult or a child "ought" to have. This in itself is largely a matter of opinion—experts on diet disagree. Since food habits play a decided role in what people eat, budget-makers then compile a food budget that will try to supply the needed caloric and nutritive values in terms of customary expenditures for foods that the people involved customarily eat. Clearly, there is considerable circularity in these com-

FIGURE 1   The Poverty Band, 1905-60 (Constant 1960 Dollars)

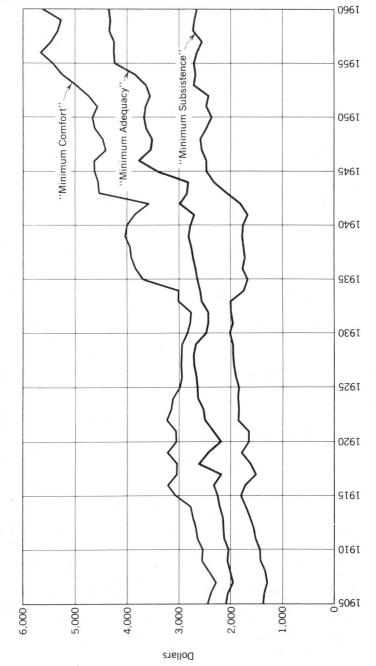

Source: Appendix 2, Table B.

putations. Families with low incomes, for instance, customarily select more beans and less meat, more hamburger and less steak, more
potatoes and less fresh corn. Income level largely determines choice;
choice determines alleged needs.

For medical care, too, budgets exhibit circularity. The poor do
not visit doctors very often. The lowest budgets therefore rely on free
medical services on an "as needed" basis. Free clinical services are
part of the accepted style of life of those on relief. Housing standards
usually prescribe minimum space per person, sanitary conditions,
heat, and other facilities. But the standards also reflect what people
at the particular income level can buy with a prescribed sum of rent
money. For clothing, minimum "needs" are based almost entirely on
actual expenditures. The criterion to a large extent is: "What is a
person at this income level accustomed to?" The budget is worked out
in terms of what the available money will buy.

Thus, standards particularize customary expenditure.

Changes in the Poverty Band

At all times, as Figure 1 demonstrates, there have persisted significant differences in what society considers sufficient. Moreover,
definitions of poverty constantly change. As the general U.S. income
level has risen, living standards have risen. Expectations have risen.
Concepts of who is poor have risen. Thus, through the years, standards of sufficiency, however defined, have generally risen. The topmost, or "minimum comfort," standard has risen rapidly—from $2,437
in 1905 to $5,609 in 1960 when valued in constant dollars of 1960 pur-
chasing power—as the average American's definition of comfort has
risen. Similarly, the intermediate level of the poverty band, that of
"minimum adequacy" standards, rose from $2,098 to $4,348 in this
period when measured in constant 1960 dollars. The "minimum subsistence" level has remained less affected by the general increase in
the economy's output and productivity. Governed mainly by the minimum amount society wishes to provide the destitute—less by expectation—it advanced in the same period, and again in constant dollars
from $1,386 to $2,662. Tables A and B of Appendix 2 spell out the
changes in the criteria of poverty, at all three levels and year by year,
in current and constant dollars respectively. Much of the upward trend
of the budget levels shown in Table A is nothing more than a downward
trend in the worth of the dollars in which they are measured, as between 1905 and 1960, consumer prices approximately tripled. This
becomes apparent when we compare Table A with Table B or with Fig-

ure 1, both of which remove the element of price changes as far as possible. Referring to Table B in the appendix, we see that the mid-point of the poverty band, in constant 1960 dollars, moved from $1,974 in 1905 to $4,206 in 1960. This better than doubling of real income expectations occurred in fits and starts over the period, and unevenly at the three "poverty" levels. It is reflected in changes in the width of the band, as well as its general upward trend, through the years. Up to the 1920's the general rise in standards was gradual and had no very marked effect on the width of the poverty band.

The narrowest portion of the band, in terms of constant 1960 dollars, occurred in 1932, when the highest-standard budgets were trimmed. Indeed, from 1922 through 1932, "minimum comfort" budgets got progressively smaller. Meantime, "subsistence" budgets rose slightly and remained fairly stable until 1933. Following the mid-1930's, the band widened out substantially. "Comfort" budgets advanced rapidly. "Subsistence" budgets fell between the Depression years 1933 and 1935, and remained low until 1943. During World War II, all budget levels rose; and the Korean War period saw another general advance. Following the Korean War, the "subsistence" level stabilized; and for several years the "minimum adequacy" and "minimum comfort" levels continued to rise.

The picture that we have here described depends in part on the assignment of individual worker budgets to various levels. Up to 1934 the Charity Organization Society budgets were assigned to the low level; thereafter, to the middle level. The C.O.S. budget used for 1935 added up to a considerably higher figure than the one it replaced. Also involved is the fact that as public assistance took over the relief work of private charities, standards set by charitable organizations began to price a different level—something closer to the "minimum adequacy" level. As a result, after the early 1930's the relief standards took over completely the lower area of the band and the budgets of charitable organizations reflected primarily the necessity to decide eligibility for free family counseling and child guidance services.

Men's Low Wages

The circularity observed in the establishment of particular budgets is present also in the aggregate notion of minimum needs which our band represents. Indeed, minimum needs are related both to the productivity of our society and to the earning patterns and levels of those recognized as working in the least skilled and lowest paid occupations.

To note this relationship we have added to the data on the poverty band
an index of men's low wages.

The data on men's low wages, shown in Table B of Appendix 2
indicate that the wages of unskilled male labor since the early 1900's
have been roughly equal to the "minimum subsistence" level of the poverty band. Since the Depression of the mid-1930's, men's low wages—
as represented by this index—have slightly exceeded this standard.
The standard, as we have said, assumes a four-member urban family
that includes a working husband, a non-working wife, and two minor
children. [1]

Men's low wages, coming to about $3,500 in 1960 before taxes,
exceed the "subsistence" level but do not equal the "adequacy" level.
Prevailing wages for men at this occupational level thus permit the
head of a household of four to maintain his family somewhat above the
relief level.

Even the average annual earnings of production workers in manufacturing in 1960, based on their average weekly rate and assuming
they worked a full year, amounted to only $4,665—just a little more
than the "minimum adequacy" budget standard of $4,348 for a family
of four in that year.

Income Shares and Shares of Poverty

There is circularity, we have noted, between needs and customary
expenditures. And customary expenditures reflect the distribution of
income. The problem of sufficiency is complicated by income shares.
The matter of income distribution thus re-enters our analysis, and
with it "relative" poverty.

As total national income rises, budgetary standards at the poverty
end of the income continuum will depend upon the degree to which the
life styles of low-income people improve. Poverty's parameters are

1. In fact many workers must have been earning somewhat less than the
amount indicated by the index used here. Data are not available for the occasional occupations — dishwasher, general laborer, waiter, etc. — which provide the bulk of the opportunities open to the very poor. This index reflects the
very lowest earnings for which some kind of consistent data could be assembled.
The basic source of information was the U. S. Bureau of Public Roads, which
supplied figures on the average hourly earnings of common laborers on federal-
aid highway projects from 1919 to 1960. Appendix 2 gives additional sources and
describes how this index compares with others. The index does not assume that
the recipient was working a normal number of hours per year; it simply indicates
what the worker earned annually on the average.

to this extent determined by the society's gross product and income
distribution. Tied closely to the most basic needs, particularly for
food, "subsistence" budgets respond slowly and feebly to general improvements in gross national product. Budgets best respond to improvements in living style as they approach the upper, or "minimum
comfort," level.

Whether those at the bottom of the income distribution are or are
not poor depends on whether their income level is or is not, by objective standards, sufficient to cover their needs. This is so even though
the standards of sufficiency themselves in turn depend both on the
amount of income available to society and on society's income distribution. Precisely because of the interdependence of objective conditions and the determination of standards of sufficiency, it is essential
to separate, as far as possible, the problem of income distribution
from that of poverty and to note in detail changes in income distribution as well as changes in standards. Of course one can deal only
with objective changes in income standards; the subjective impact of
changes in income structure is beyond this study. All we can say is
that while one man says, "My neighbor has more and I am thereby
richer," another man says, "My neighbor has more and I am thereby
poorer." That an individual's sense of happiness is dependent not only
on his own level of consumption but also on what his neighbor consumes
has long been known; but besides suggesting a certain "rationality" of
"dog in the manger" type actions, this knowledge does not help us much.

Knowledge about changes in income distribution is still far from
definitive. There is dissatisfaction with the data, difficulty of selection among available data, and a multiplicity of measurement concepts.
Still, the field of income distribution need no longer cause one to be-
moan the "deplorable dearth of information";[1] on the contrary, careful
empirical work has been carried out to fill what was, until just before
World War II, a major void. Indeed, the qualitative and quantitative
contributions to this literature by American economists are most impressive.

As the condition of poverty is here identified as the gap between
needs and "command over goods and services," income needs careful
definition. The standard definition of income for the analysis of personal income is that used by the Office of Business Economics in the
Department of Commerce.[2]

1. Frank Streightoff, The Distribution of Income in the United States, Columbia University Press, New York, 1912, p. 152.

2. It is related to the family as a recipient unit and represents current income
before income taxes; it is measured in terms of the sum of wages and salary re-

In measuring the inequality of income in the United States, the reference point is never a posited ideal of absolute equality, but one that relates to earlier times and other countries. It is commonly asserted that incomes in the United States are now less unequally distributed than in the past or in most of the rest of the world. Summarizing the evidence on the income changes between 1929 and the present, Heilbroner observes: "A striking change meets the eye. Something like a huge social escalation process, a massive migration upwards through the income strata, has taken place. ... What we see in this ... panorama is clearly not just a static comparison. It is a pair of balance sheets which testifies to a ... wholesome vertical shift of living standards."[1]

This conclusion, generally agreed upon by most economists until 1960, is based primarily on the detailed statistical work of Simon Kuznets and Selma Goldsmith.[2] Their studies actually tell us more and in

---

ceipts (net of social insurance contributions) and all other money income, including transfer payments, such as unemployment insurance receipts. In addition, family income covers imputed non-money items, such as the net value of food and fuel produced and consumed by farm operators' families and the net rental value of owner-occupied homes. In 1950 the non-money items accounted for 5 per cent of the family personal income total and while no recent study is available it is probable that this proportion has decreased since that date. Indications are that the non-money incomes are mostly concentrated at the lower end of the distribution, particularly in the agricultural sector and in some low-wage service industries.

This definition of income has been widely used and is the one most generally accepted. It is the one used in the Goldsmith study, which provides us with most of what we know about income distribution in the United States, and is also the one used in the computations of the present study. Although not sufficient to answer fully all the questions about income distribution generally posed, it is a useful concept for appraising the degree of income inequality at a given point of time and only slightly less useful for appraising changes over time, particularly long-term changes. It is used here to survey the central question of the equality of the income distribution in the United States.

See "Income Distribution in the United States by Size, 1944-1950," Office of Business Economics, Department of Commerce, 1953. See also, for the use of income data in this study, Appendix III.

1. Robert Heilbroner, The Future as History, Harper and Brothers, New York, 1959, pp. 122-23.

2. Simon Kuznets, "Shares of Upper Income Groups in Incomes and Savings," Occasional Paper No. 35, National Bureau of Economic Research, New York, 1950; and Selma Goldsmith, George Jaszi, Hyman Kaitz and Maurice Liebenberg, "Size Distribution of Income Since the Mid-Thirties," The Review of Economics and Statistics, February 1954, pp. 1-32.

greater detail about the changes in the shares of income of those at the higher income levels than those at the lower levels and indicate little, if anything, in detail about a change at the lower levels. Changes in income distribution are studied by ranking the total population according to their income, dividing it into quintiles (fifths) or, for the top, into smaller groups, and examining the changes in their relative shares of total personal income.

In this fashion Appendix 4 shows the distribution of income according to quintiles for selected years. The years 1941 and 1947 illustrate the prewar income distribution and the postwar peak; the year 1953 seems to start a reverse trend in income inequality. In Appendix 4 the year 1953 has consequently been chosen as an anchor year for splitting the 1935/36 to 1959 period into two sub-periods. This subdivision has the advantage of illuminating the most recent developments.

The "huge social escalation" that has taken place does not show decreases in income inequality; it hinges on the massive improvement in the society's real wealth, on its essentially productive performance. The escalator image is accurate. The rich and poor have continued to "keep their distances" while the entire structure has shifted to a higher plane. The first part is illustrated by the appendix table as well as by the fact that in 1940 the top 5 per cent of U.S. families received about 25 per cent of all incomes and in 1961 this group still received about 20 per cent. The second is confirmed by the observation that the real per capita income of the average American non-farm family in 1960 was almost as high as the real per capita income of the wealthiest 5 per cent in 1940. What has happened is that the problem of poverty, because of a very real social escalation, has slipped away from under the neat and reasonable theoretical formulation which equated the problem of poverty with the problem of income distribution. One might almost say that the economic base has moved out from under the theoretical superstructure, leaving the analysis in theoretical limbo.

There is also no evidence that whatever limited decrease in the inequality of incomes has occurred can be associated with the workings of a high-level economy. Indeed, the most significant shift toward greater equality took place under very abnormal conditions, the Depression and the Second World War. The Depression pulled the rug out from under everyone and, in many cases, those with more lost more; World War II brought unprecedented levels of employment and provided increased income for many not normally in the labor force. Sobering also is the fact that since the end of the Korean conflict (1953), the shift toward equality has stopped or slowed down.

2

Life styles at the "need" levels of the poverty band

SOCIETY'S general consensus that a family of four earning in 1960 less than $2,662 was living below "minimum subsistence" is significant in trying to define U.S. poverty. Society judges that a family of the same size should be able to live at the level of "adequacy" on $4,348 per year or in "minimum comfort" on $5,609 per year. This is the judgment derived from the budgets studied and discussed earlier. Such is the contemporary "poverty band" or continuum of agreed-upon "needs."

To develop a more concrete picture of standards, the New School study went to the actual quantities of food and other necessities in these recommended budgets, in order to visualize the varying life styles of the U.S. poor, past and present. Exact comparisons are difficult. Except for food, the budgetary differences, both between levels of sufficiency and between years, do not lie merely in a simple listing of items. To be meaningful, the quality and variety of goods would also have to be determined.

Purpose

In surveying the components of each of the budgets studied—and more than sixty were studied for most years—the New School poverty staff discovered another significant circularity; namely, that the purposes for which the standards are set tend to determine the budgets, both their composition and money level.

Budgets to determine needs at the "subsistence" level were constructed mainly to establish eligibility for public assistance. The mid-level standards, those termed "fair," were constructed primarily to determine a "living wage" and, more recently, are used by community service societies to decide whether families needing and requesting counseling and guidance should pay for it or not. The higher level budgets, generally termed "minimum comfort," on the other hand have in common only the fact that none was constructed for relief purposes. Of this latter group, many were used in settling wage disputes—mostly of skilled workers or civil service workers—or were constructed to measure costs and changes in costs of maintaining a commonly accepted standard of living without reference to a particular wage or relief action.

The life styles so set, and the derived notion of poverty or deprivation—in the apparent objectivity of a package of specific needs—reflect society's judgments of differences in social function and status. In practice the minimum which a family needs to maintain physical efficiency is ascertained by surveying what families actually buy. The separating of minimum needs of those on relief from those who use the community agencies for non-money services is done by asking what the latter have and what they spend it on.

Changes in Budget Content

Appendix 3 presents comparisons of major items in typical budgets of the first, third, and sixth decades of the present century. Standards of 1908, 1935, and 1960 are compared at each of the three "poverty band" levels. Again a four-person family is assumed.

For foods, the long-term and inter-budget differences are striking. The low budgets generally give more emphasis to low-price, starchy foods than to high-protein foods. This relationship is traced in line 6 of the appendix table. Housing facilities as budgeted reflect contemporary cost and the availability of housing, and thus the circularity of standards discussed earlier. The principal difference in recommended housing facilities appears in standards other than the amount of space— that is, in sanitary conditions, state of repair, and so on. The change over time in these recommended facilities is more marked than the difference in expenditure level, especially in budgets of the "comfort" type.

Most significant is the ratio of food and housing to total expenditure. Items other than food and housing—such as clothing, household furniture, household operation, personal care, recreation—took 18 cents of every dollar at the lowest budget level and 31 cents at the highest budget level in 1908 (see line 9 of the table). In 1960 these items accounted for 25 cents at the "subsistence" level, and almost 50 cents in the "minimum comfort" budget. As time passed, society agreed that the minima should increasingly involve more than filling a belly and obtaining a roof.

Content of 1960 Budgets

Typical of 1960 "subsistence" level budgets is a New York City budget requiring an income of $2,660. It provides for simple clothing to protect against the weather and maintain cleanliness. It leaves no room for impulse buying or fashion. It barely copes with the problem of wear. A woman's coat, for instance, must last five years. Leftover food must be retrieved. There can be no error. A cup of flour spilled means no thickening that week; a blown bulb, no light for that month; and a chair broken in anger cannot be replaced for a year. The meat budget allows for stewing lamb, beef liver or heart, picnic shoulder, fillet of haddock, or perhaps a boned veal roast. No frozen foods are provided for. Compared to a 1935 "subsistence" budget in New York City, which provided $600 less in 1960 dollars, the 1960 budget emphasizes more fresh vegetables and high-protein foods. It still allows for only 520 carfares, as the 1935 budget did, and allows nothing for an occasional glass of beer, tobacco, or telephone calls.

The budget assumes a small rented five-room flat (two or three rooms more than in 1935). The family living room might have two chairs. A mattress and spring on legs may serve as a couch. A dropleaf table for eating, two straight chairs may also be there. Linoleum may cover the floor, and there can be a lamp or two. Electricity is to be used carefully. An electric refrigerator and iron are allowed (neither was provided for in 1935). The family may listen to the radio an hour a day; but television is not included in the budget. There will be money to buy aspirin but none for "miracle" drugs. The husband may get a haircut once a month, and the wife a home permanent once a year. She can use a self-service launderette. There will be no money to buy the children candy or ice cream, or to go to the movies, or to offer a visitor a cup of coffee.

With 1960's typical "minimum adequacy" budget—taking one valued at $4,460 in New York City as typical—the family may add some ground chuck to the weekly diet. It may have beef instead of lamb stew. A stewing chicken may be substituted for beef heart. Twice as much may be spent for high-protein foods as for farinaceous foods. The rented five-room apartment (four rooms in 1935 in a similar WPA budget for U.S. cities) can have an upholstered chair and a large cotton rug, even end tables. A clean, individual bathroom is allowed. The family may own an electric toaster, vacuum cleaner, and fan, and have a minimum-service family telephone. The teenager may go to the movies once a month, the adults every three weeks. Once a year the family may go to a sporting event or concert. With persistent wisdom in spending, there will be money for a fifty-mile vacation trip by rail to the country, a daily newspaper, some paperback books or magazines, cigarets, occasional home entertainment of friends, and Christmas and birthday gifts. The wife and children may occasionally ride public transportation. The budget makes no allocation for television or for a car.

Such is the "minimum adequacy" budget today—some $1,700 more in 1960 dollars than the comparable WPA budget of 1935.

Under the "minimum comfort" budget as outlined in the U. S. Bureau of Labor Statistics' Interim City Worker's Family Budget for 1959 in New York City, the family must have an income of $5,400 in 1960 dollars. At this level there is, in effect, a margin of choice. Once a month, the family might buy a steak. Three times as much may be spent for high-protein food as for floury foods. A cake mix may be used occasionally, and frozen orange juice may be had. There is money for tobacco or an occasional can of beer. Sometimes snacks may be bought away from home. The five-room apartment need never get colder than seventy degrees. A wool rug may cover the parlor floor. A sofa may replace the spring-and-mattress couch. The family may make a few out-of-town phone calls. A television set may be bought on the installment plan. The family may buy a used car every three years and take a week's camping trip each summer. It may own a cheap camera.

This is the living style that the Bureau of Labor Statistics calls "modest but adequate." On this level, the family is spending more than twice as much as the contemporary family receiving Aid to Dependent Children or relief in New York City, and about $1,700 more in 1960 dollars than it would have spent in the 1935 "minimum comfort" budget of the University of California's Heller Committee.

Range of Today's Budget Standards

Standards of sufficiency, we have noted, vary in the present as they did in the past. The broad pattern of these differences is apparent from Figure 1 and the basic appendix tables. However, the band traced in Figure 1 represents the average for each type of budget studied and understates the width of the poverty band at any particular time. In each year, we have taken a single budget figure at each of the three levels of the band, whereas in fact there is in any year more than one budget of the "minimum subsistence" or the "minimum adequacy" or the "minimum comfort" type.

At one extreme, the "subsistence" level, the average U.S. cost standard for a four-person family receiving Aid to Dependent Children grants under the state-federal public assistance program in the early

1960's was about $2,150 per year. This was for a family consisting
of an incapacitated father, a mother, a boy of 11 and a girl of 7. At
the other extreme, the "minimum comfort" standard published by the
Heller Committee of the University of California came to a total of
$6,087, or to $5,464 after taxes. This defined the "commonly accepted
wage-earner standard of living." The 1959 Bureau of Labor Statistics'
Interim City Worker's Family Budget—similar in purpose and use—
averaged about the same. Thus the "comfort" budgets in 1960 called
for more than twice the amount of the average relief budget. They
were almost four times as high as the lowest ADC standard. Ranging
in between were various budgets used by community council agencies.

Beyond the dollar variations in contemporary notions of sufficiency
there is much geographical variation in the "subsistence" standard, in
programs of Aid to Dependent Children. These ADC programs now
constitute the major portion of federal grants-in-aid. The incomes
stipulated, state by state, show how differently administrators define
even the abject poor. In the practice of actual disbursement are other
variations as well. In some states, families are entitled to the entire
difference between their actual income and the minimum standards.
In others only a predetermined percentage of the difference between
minimum standard and actual income is paid, and some states fix an
absolute maximum regardless of family size. In still other states, aid
is not granted to those who have savings or capital of more than specified amounts, or relatives to help them.

Tabulations prepared from 1958 data give the figures for ADC families with four members.[1] The "minimum subsistence" budget, as defined by the five states with the lowest ADC standards, averaged $1,600;
for the five highest it averaged $2,700. The range in stipulated "sub-
sistence" levels is widened in practice by the fact that administrative
restrictions leading to lower payments tend to be found among states
with lower standards.

Part, but only a small part, of the range in the ADC standards
may represent geographic differences in the cost of living. Indeed, the
states with the lowest dollar standards are in the South, where the cost
of living is somewhat lower. There is also a tendency to establish
standards in line with payments actually made. Payments seem to reflect more the states' financial limitations, and here again the South
fares poorly. In general, the northeastern and the northwestern states
have more liberal standards. Also, while almost 100 per cent of need

1.   "Monthly Cost Standards for Basic Needs Used by States for Assistance
Budgets," U. S. Department of Health, Education, and Welfare, Social Security
Administration, Division of Program Statistics and Analysis, August 1959.

as defined in the state budgets is met in the actual payments in the
northeast, less than 70 per cent of the defined standards is met in the
payments in the South. [1]

The lowest group of five states assigns about 53 per cent of the total budget to food; one low state assigned as much as 63 per cent. The
highest group assigns about 42 per cent. The lowest states allot 19 per
cent to rent, while the highest group allots 28 per cent. Clothing requirements show less variation than food standards. But personal in-
cidentals are viewed as a need to which $257 per year is allocated in
one state and nothing in another. Medical requirements are treated by
most states as "special" and often given in kind. At least two-thirds
of the states view the item "medicine chest" as a basic need, for which
an average of $108 is budgeted. One-third of the states budget for some
variant of a prepaid group-contract medical plan. The higher-standard
states typically provide also for one or more "other needs." However,
it is unusual for even liberal standards to include, for instance, a recreation allowance. Many other goods and services are considered
"special" needs. Each state specifies what these are. The fact that
the higher-standard states list more of these special needs further wid-
ens the range.

The variation in ADC standards of sufficiency thus makes it clear
that regional differences enlarge very substantially the range of the
poverty band. The widened band underlines once again the appropri-
ateness of the observation of Marshall, an economist who knew nothing
of the affluent society:

> The term "Necessaries" ... has been used elliptically, the
> subject to which it refers being left to be supplied by the reader;
> and since the implied subject has varied, the reader has often
> supplied one which the writer did not intend and thus misunder-
> stood his drift.... A more careful analysis has made it evident
> that there is for each rank of industry, at any time and place, a
> more or less clearly defined income which is necessary for merely
> sustaining its members; while there is another and larger income
> which is necessary for keeping it in full efficiency.... With this
> understanding we may say that the income would in the course of
> time produce a more than proportionate increase in their effi-
> ciency.... [2]

1. Ellen J. Perkins, "Unmet Need in Public Assistance," Social Security
Bulletin, April 1960, pp. 3-11.

2. Alfred Marshall, Principles of Economics, Book II, Chapter III, C.W.
Guillebaud, ed., 9th ed., Macmillan, London, 1961, pp. 68-69.

Life Styles and the Concept of Poverty

The budgetary minima described above to convey the "life styles" of the poor do not imply that the poor actually live in the manner the budgets suggest. The reality of life, particularly for the abject poor, is startlingly different. Instead of the severe rationality of choices posited by the budgets, we find what might appear as its opposite.

Description of the way of life of the poor is not our task. Others have done it and have done it well.[1] The way in which the life of the poor differs from that posited by the budgets does not invalidate the usefulness of the money income equivalent so arrived at. What is significant is not the presence of the battered and used television set, or the perpetually operated transistor radio not contemplated by the budget-makers but the fact, discussed in detail later, that the monetary equivalents connected with the minimum standards provide cut-off levels separating different groups of people.

The survey of practice in determining needs has shown as great a variation as a priori arguments about the meaning of poverty. This variation is due primarily to the fact that establishing who is poor is more than an exercise in description. Most people who say that a man is poor imply that he should not be. Statements about the existence, extent, and distribution of poverty are actually statements about the existence, extent, and distribution of a set of problems. In an affluent society, poverty, in its very essence, reflects a posture of social policy.

Operationally meaningful formulations of social policy call for the translation of essentially subjective and temporal perceptions into standardized notions. To bridge the problems of consensus, levels of "minimum subsistence," "adequacy" and "comfort" have been introduced by those concerned with the implementation of specific programs aimed at making the poor non-poor.

The band of poverty sketched in the previous section is more useful as a tool of analysis than as an index of consensus. Formulating different levels of need follows from recognizing the variety of courses of action. There is no single definition of need because poverty is not a single thing. There is no single definition of poverty because poverty is not a single condition.

1. For vivid description, see the work of Julius Horowitz, The Inhabitants, World, Cleveland, 1960, for New York City; Facts, Fallacies and Future, the Greenleigh Associates Report, n.d., on the ADC program in Chicago; Louisa Shotwell, The Harvester, Doubleday, New York, 1961, for the migrant workers; or Tent City, by the Industrial Union Department, AFL-CIO, Washington, n.d., for the southern rural Negro.

The selection of different levels in the band of poverty to identify the groups of concern to policy-makers leads to the exclusion of other groups. Through analysis of the causes of poverty of those included, policy action is influenced. Later it will be seen that individuals defined as poor by the three levels of the band are different from the rest of society in their demographic, social, and psychological profiles. Policies aimed at the amelioration of the conditions of each group have thus both different goals and different potential beneficiaries.

3

The count of the poor

AS NOTED, contemporary practice in public and private agencies points to three clusters of dollar equivalents for national minimum needs: "minimum subsistence"—$2,662 per year for a family of four in 1960 (to use the exact figure calculated in our poverty band); "minimum adequacy"—$4,348; and "minimum comfort"—$5,609. From such differences in judgment stem the many recent and varied estimates of the number of poor in the United States.

The author of one well-known survey of poverty analyzes the different means used to estimate the extent of poverty. He observes that "there is no point in getting involved in an endless methodological controversy over the precise point at which a family become impoverished." While there is ground for disagreement, he says, "whatever the precise calibrations, it is obvious that these statistics represent an enormous, an unconscionable amount of human suffering in this land. They should be read with a sense of outrage."[1] The purpose of the author of these comments was to arouse moral indignation. Indignation is a necessary starting point if anything useful is to be done about minimizing poverty. Concern about poverty is not enough, however. To deal with poverty calls for definition and specification. To withhold specification, to refuse to search for statistically verifiable risk and causation is to betray.

Using the three income levels charted in Figure 1 and relating them to studies on income distribution, the New School poverty study staff arrived at estimates of the number of poor in the United States since 1929 by contemporary standards. The figures appear in Appendix 5. In making this count, the dollar equivalents of the "subsistence," "adequacy," and "comfort" standards were adjusted to allow for variations through time in average family size and for the needs of unattached individuals.

---

1. Michael Harrington, The Other America: Poverty in the United States, Macmillan, New York, 1962, appendix.

In 1960, our figures show, almost 20 million persons lived in conditions at least as bad as those described by reference to the "minimum subsistence" budgets; 46 million lived under conditions below those described in terms of the "minimum adequacy" budgets; and 71 million lived at a standard described as being less than that of "minimum comfort." Of all households (consumer units) in the United States, by this count, 11 per cent fell below the "subsistence" budget standard in 1960, 26 per cent below the "adequacy" standard, and 40 per cent below the "comfort" standard (Appendix 5).

Changes Through Time

How has the number of poor changed since prewar years? The change can be measured, first of all, by taking a count for a series of years of the number who failed to meet the standards of sufficiency prevailing at the time, with these standards expressed in then current dollar values. Such a count, made in the New School poverty study, is illustrated in the first part of Figure 2. Here we trace, through three decades, the numbers of persons falling below the three levels used in this study, according to the then existing standards evaluated in current dollars. We see that, by this measure, there were fewer poor in 1960

FIGURE 2   Number of Persons Below Three Budget Levels in Selected Years, by Contemporary Standards and by 1960 Standards

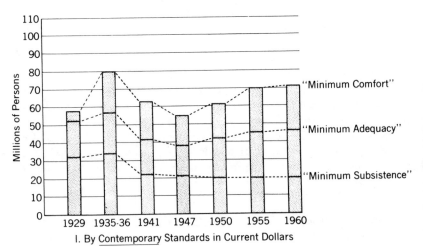

I. By Contemporary Standards in Current Dollars

than in 1929 by low- and middle-level budget definitions but more when
the "minimum comfort" definition is used. In three decades, 12 million people—though, of course, not necessarily the same people—were
lifted out of the worst poverty. But there were in 1960, by the same
measure, 71 million people below the currently defined "comfort" level,
compared with 58 million in 1929. Evidently many of those who, so to
speak, rose out of yesterday's stark poverty entered the areas above
subsistence but below present-day standards of healthful, decent living.
    A simple count does not, however, take into consideration the
growth of population through the years. In order to relate the trends
to population size, the New School poverty study staff made similar
measurements in terms of percentages, in this case of households or
"consumer units." As Figure 3 shows, the percentage of households
living at each of the three budget levels used in this study has decreased
somewhat since 1929. Although many people still live below "subsistence," the decrease in the proportion of households below that standard
has been particularly steady and striking, despite the increased cost of
living. This is partly because there has been less growth in administratively determined "subsistence" budgets than in the "minimum" comfort budgets. Also involved is the fact that prior to the mid-forties
most families were dependent upon one breadwinner only. It is estimated that in 1929, for instance, 62 per cent of American families had

FIGURE 2 (Continued)

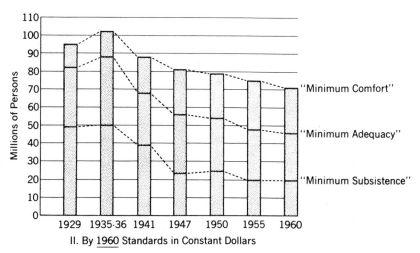

II. By 1960 Standards in Constant Dollars

Source: Appendix 5, Table B.

FIGURE 3   Per Cent of Households Below Three
            Budget Levels in Selected Years, by
            Contemporary Standards in Current Dollars

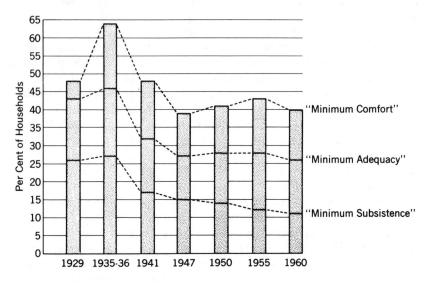

Source: Appendix 5, Table A.

only one source of income. By 1960 this proportion of families had
fallen to 46 per cent.[1] In the 1960's, women's participation in the labor force generally means two pay checks per family. The probability
of extreme poverty is thus somewhat less among low-paid workers'
families.

The changes over the years in the incidence of poverty can be
measured in another way—by projecting present standards back to earlier years. This the New School poverty study staff also did, using a
simple monetary deflation of 1960 standards in order to rule out changes in the value of the dollar. The results of these computations are
shown graphically in the second part of Figure 2. In each of the years
shown on the chart (except 1955, and then only at the level of "subsistence"), there were more persons living below today's standard than below the contemporary historical standard.

1. Data for 1929 from Maurice Leven, Harold Moulton and Clark Warburton,
America's Capacity to Consume, The Brookings Institution, Washington, 1934,
p. 236; data for 1960 from Current Population Reports, Bureau of the Census,
Series P60-6 and P60-37.

Thus, if we project today's operational definitions of poverty back to an earlier period, it appears that more people three decades ago were "poor" than were considered to be poor at the time. And, quite evidently, if we were to use the standards of thirty years ago and project them forward to today, we would find that "poverty" had decidedly dwindled. Either exercise tells us more about changing standards than about those judged to be poor by their fellow citizens.

It is in this context that the notion of relativity as applied to poverty over time shows all its shortcomings. To say that poverty is relative is not helpful to society. If comparisons from one period to another are to be made, the New School study staff feels they should be made in terms of contemporary standards.

Other Estimates of the Number of Poor

As we noted in Section 1, estimates of the extent of poverty in the United States have been made in recent years by the Conference on Economic Progress, the University of Michigan Survey Research Center, Gabriel Kolko, and Robert Lampman. Their findings are summarized in Table 1, where they are compared, as appropriate, to our "adequacy" and "comfort" estimates: none of the three studies attempted to measure the proportion of relief-eligible households.

Lampman and Kolko, both using essentially the same data and techniques, came to the separate conclusions that in 1957, 21 per cent of U.S. households (Lampman) or 27.5 per cent (Kolko) were poor. Their differences rest almost entirely with different definitions of poverty, described in Section 1. Kolko's 27.5 per cent for 1957 represents those households living in poverty, by his criterion, while the additional 16.5 per cent shown in Table 1 as below "minimum comfort" are those existing in "a shadowy area ranging from poverty to hard-pressed insecurity." The dollar figures for a family of four in these studies were as usual adjusted to suit the average needs of unrelated individuals and different-sized families.[1] Using still other criteria, also described in Section 1, the Michigan study estimated that 20 per cent of all families, and 28 per cent of all "adult units," were living in poverty in 1959.

Earlier it was pointed out that standards of poverty have changed through time, and that comparisons from one period to another are affected by changes in standards. Small wonder, then, that in addition to disagreement about how many poor there now are, there is disagreement about how many poor there were in the past.

1. Lampman, op. cit., p. 5; Kolko, op. cit., p. 102.

TABLE 1   Five Estimates of the Proportion of Households Living
Below Minimum Standards, Selected Years

Year	Study	Below "Minimum Adequacy"	Below "Minimum Comfort"[a]
1947	Conference on Economic Progress	39	67
	Gabriel Kolko	33	51
	Robert J. Lampman	28	--
	This study	28	40
1957	Gabriel Kolko	27	44
	Robert J. Lampman	21	--
	This study	27	41
1959	Morgan—University of Michigan	28[b]	38
	This study	28	44
1960	Conference on Economic Progress	26	48
	This study	27[c]	41

Sources: Conference on Economic Progress, Poverty and Deprivation in the United States, Washington, 1962; James N. Morgan, Martin H. David, Wilbur J. Cohen and Harvey E. Brazer, Income and Welfare in the United States (University of Michigan, Survey Research Center), McGraw-Hill, New York, 1962; Gabriel Kolko, Wealth and Power in America, Praeger, New York, 1962; Robert J. Lampman, "The Low Income Population and Economic Growth," Study Paper No. 12, U.S. Congress, Joint Economic Committee, 1959. Figures shown for our study do not agree with those in Appendix 5, Table A, since we did not apply the same adjustments here in order to keep our figures comparable to the other series shown in this table.
    a. Comparable to Kolko's "insecurity" and the CEP's "deprivation."
    b. Adult units.
    c. Proportion of adult units (of which there are more than consumer units in the population) used here for comparability.

A dramatic illustration of the effects of changing standards is provided by comparative studies made in England. In Section 1 it was noted that in 1899 Rowntree calculated that 10 per cent of the people of York were living in what he defined as "primary poverty." In 1936 York was revisited and 4 per cent of the families in the city were found by Rowntree to be in "primary poverty" by the 1899 definition. However, he did not use the 1899 definition as his principal reference, but changed the definition through a new study of worker spending. According to the 1936 definition, 17.7 per cent of the population of York was found to be poor. In 1950 a third survey was made, at which time 2.7 per cent of the families were poor by the 1936 definition. This would

suggest that by 1899 standards, there were virtually no poor in York
at mid-century. [1]

Like Rowntree, three of the recent investigations of poverty referred to above made time comparisons. Unlike Rowntree, who judged
York in 1899 by 1899 standards and in 1936 by 1936 standards, they did
not make a comparison by contemporary standards. Lampman and
Kolko projected the standards of the late 1940's forward and found a
smaller proportion of poor in the United States in the late 1950's.
Adopting the higher, more recent standards of the late 1950's, on the
other hand, the Conference on Economic Progress, looking backward,
found a very large decrease since 1947 in both proportion of households
and number of poor. Essentially, Lampman and Kolko projected old
standards forward whereas the Conference on Economic Progress applied the higher standards of recent times to the past. As will be seen
from Table 1, the poverty study staff data, with changing standards,
indicate less than a one per cent decrease in the proportion of households living below the "adequacy" and "comfort" levels over the ten-
year span 1947 to 1957, though they did show a considerable decrease
in the proportion below contemporary "subsistence" levels.

These changes must be judged against the background of a clear
improvement in productivity, in the level of disposable income, and in
the general well-being of our society. In the face of marked progress
in the rest of society, the poor remain, by contemporary standards, a
consistently large group—a blight on the nation's record.

1. B. Seebohm Rowntree and G. R. Lavers, Poverty and the Welfare State:
A Third Social Survey of York Dealing Only with Economic Questions, Longmans,
Green and Co., London, 1951.
    A. L. Bowley and Margaret H. Hogg, in Has Poverty Diminished?, London,
1925, surveyed the incidence of poverty in a number of other towns between 1912
and 1924, with comparable results.

PART TWO

4

The risk of poverty

INVESTIGATORS have often classified poverty under three main headings: collective poverty, individual poverty, and group poverty.

Collective poverty, the poverty of entire economies, is characteristic of the globe and of most of recorded history. The vast majority of countries have had difficulty in all periods of making resources meet needs. This is the poverty with which economists have traditionally been concerned.

At the same time, in the Anglo-Saxon tradition poverty has often been considered individual in nature. Echoing and misreading the writings of the classical economists, many, particularly in America, have argued that poverty is the result of improvidence, drunkenness, and sloth. More recently this kind of individual poverty has been called "case poverty," implying an individual's own and peculiar marginality. That such poverty exists in contemporary America cannot be denied.

Since the first Factory Acts were passed in England in the early nineteenth century, another view has developed: many came to see poverty as the consequence of the imperfection of the industrial system. As well as bringing plenty for some, industrialism is viewed as bringing involuntary poverty for many. It is perceived that men can become impoverished through technological unemployment, through recurrent business crises, through their weak bargaining position in seeking a living wage; in sum, the malallocation of resources is viewed as at the heart of poverty. Woman and child labor laws, social security legislation, minimum-wage laws, unemployment insurance schemes, fair labor practices acts, price support schemes, the Employment Act of 1946 represent efforts by U.S. society to counteract the imperfections of the industrial system. Because of these efforts the economic and industrial system better meets the needs of men. In some situations, the imperfections of the market bear directly on contemporary poverty. But on the whole we find contemporary poverty not to be the result of widespread imperfections in the society's economic mechanism.

Unlike the collective poverty of entire societies and the individual

poverty of some, contemporary poverty is predominantly the poverty
of specific groups. The fact that statistics of poverty are presented
in terms of either "incidence" or "composition" indicates that this was
always so to some degree. In contemporary America, if one belongs
to certain groups—characterized, for instance, by age, sex, race,
place of residence—the risk of poverty is great. In contemporary
America, one's statistical chances of being poor are considerably
above the average if one is, for example, over 65, a female head of
household, non-white, or a rural farm resident. Data assembled in
the New School study show how U.S. poverty increasingly involves individuals and families almost exclusively with these "poverty-linked
characteristics."

The Gross Association

What percentage of families and unattached individuals with specific attributes are poor? How many of the poor have these attributes?
To answer these questions we first studied the 1960 relationship
of a dozen social and demographic characteristics to three low-income
levels. The lowest income level, representing extreme poverty, was
that under $500, the middle level was that under $2,000, and the highest, that under $4,500. The characteristics (of the family head where
applicable) which we studied were:

Non-white
Female
65 years of age or over
14 to 24 years of age
Rural farm residence
Southern residence: White and non-white together
                               Non-white alone
No work experience
Part-time experience: All with only part-time experience
                                Those with 0–26 weeks
                                Those with 27–49 weeks
Families with six or more children under 18 years of age
Less than eight years of schooling

All these characteristics showed a clear, significant, strong association with low income (Appendix 7). And the association is under-
stated in the figures since comparisons are made with the total population, which includes groups possessing these characteristics. Had
people possessing these characteristics been compared with people not
possessing them, the contrast would be even more striking.

Compared to all families, a greater proportion of those with the specified characteristics had less than $500 income. Almost without exception, possession of any one such characteristic doubled or considerably more than doubled the risk of abject poverty. Whereas, for example, 2.5 per cent of all families in 1960 had income below $500, 6.2 per cent of families headed by a person with less than eight years of schooling had income less than this amount. Only very youthful and aged families did not deviate much from the percentage of all families with less than $500 income. Payments under the Old Age Assistance program, Social Security benefits, public and private pensions, and savings had insured by 1960 that only three aged families out of a hundred needed to try to live on an income of less than $500 per year.

At the $2,000 income level, the situation changes. At this level, Social Security and Old Age Assistance no longer provide a floor under which income cannot fall. The gap between aged families and families in general has widened; only 13 per cent of all American families had income under $2,000 in 1960 as compared with 31 per cent for aged families. The same widening of the gap holds for non-white families, for those headed by a person with only part-time work experience or none at all, and also for families whose head had no more than eight years of schooling.

At the $4,500 income level, all of the characteristics studied play a part in keeping family incomes below that level. Indeed, more than half of the families with any one of these traits had less than $4,500 in income in 1960, while less than 37 per cent of all families were in this situation.

Unattached individuals with the same characteristics run similarly high risks of being poor. One special feature is added. As the appendix table makes clear, being an unattached individual is itself an attribute linked to low income: whereas, for instance, 2.5 per cent of American families had income of less than $500 in 1960, 14.6 per cent of the unattached were in that class.

As one moves up the income scale, the data show that the demographic and social composition of income classes changes. At the low end, many characteristics are very pronounced, whereas in the upper ranges their incidence is quite modest. Starting from the low end of the income scale, the New School poverty study staff traced the social and demographic composition in 1960 of each income class up to the $4,500-$5,000 bracket and compared it with that of the total population. The data are presented in Appendix 6. In that table the percentage of all non-white families in 1960 (9.5), for instance, is compared with the percentage of families in the income bracket $0-$500 that were non-white (21.7). Similar relationships are shown for seven characteristics and ten income classes. Then the percentages for each income bracket

FIGURE 4 Incidence of Seven Characteristics, by Income Class, 1960

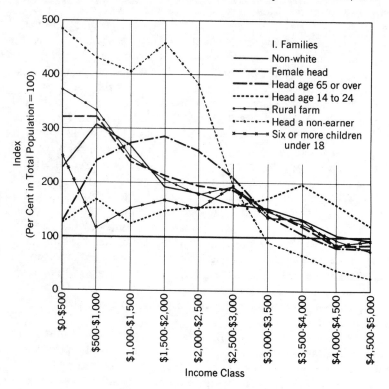

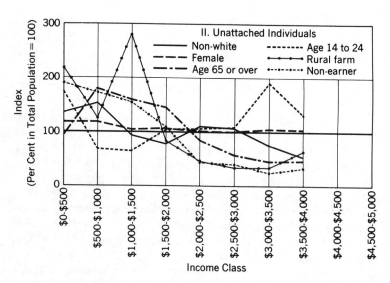

Source: Appendix 6.

are added to yield a "cumulative poverty profile." This measure has
no relationship to the actual numbers of families involved, as the characteristics may overlap in the same person or family. Taking, for example, the cumulative percentage for all families, the figure 55.8 indicates that if families with any of the specified characteristics had
only one such characteristic, then nearly 56 in 100 families would be
so identifiable. It is, of course, more reasonable to infer that a significant number of families have two or more of these characteristics.
Such an inference is even more reasonable for families in low income
brackets, as is obvious when we see that in the income bracket $0-$500
the cumulative percentage of families having any one of these characteristics was 148, against a cumulative percentage of 56 for families
in general. To facilitate comparison, the cumulative percentages are
then transposed, in the last line of the table, into index numbers with
100 as the value for all families. The same calculations are presented
separately in this table for unattached individuals.

Figure 4 traces graphically the separate income impact of these
characteristics. The points on this chart are derived by reading hori-
zontally the figures in the base table and transposing them to index
numbers with the weight of each characteristic among all families (and,
separately, all unattached individuals) equal to 100. Similarly, Fig-

FIGURE 5   Cumulative Incidence of Seven
                  Characteristics, by Income Class, 1960

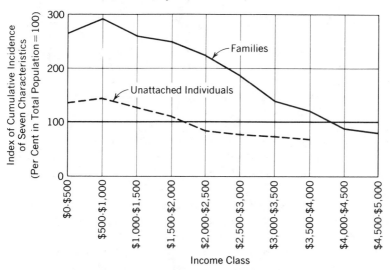

Source: Appendix 6. The characteristics (of family head where applicable)
are: non-white; female; age 65 or over; age 14 to 24; rural farm residence; non-
earner; and, for families only, six or more children under 18.

ure 5 is a graphic representation of the cumulative poverty profile on
an income basis which Appendix 6 yields.

From these two charts a clear pattern emerges. The income
bracket in which the characteristics most clearly resemble those in
all families is $4,000-$4,500; for unattached individuals, it is $2,000=
$2,500. These levels can be viewed as turning points, as poverty cut-
off levels. The chart also shows that, in the case of families, the
$3,000 of yearly income often used as separating the poor from the non-
poor is spurious. At this level of income the proportion of families
with the demographic characteristics of the poor is high: witness the
bunching of the lines at the 160 index level. These calculations highlight how contemporary poverty is isolated more clearly when viewed
as a departure from a demographic than from an income norm.

Through most of the economic history of the United States low income and poverty characterized a considerable part of the population.
The old and the young, male and female, farmer and city dweller,
black and white, northerner and southerner, almost all shared in the
national insufficiency; if one were black or a female family head or
southern, the risk of poverty was greater but not much greater, as
many without these attributes were also poor. The postwar situation
is quite another story. As its over-all impact was lessened, poverty
became increasingly a burden carried by select groups.

Earlier it had been important to note, as Scott Fitzgerald did in
the twenties, that the rich were different in ways other than their having money. Being rich meant, in addition, a different way of life, a
different perception of reality. It was the characteristic of the individuals carried over to the group that made the rich different. But
aside from the very rich, differences in income did not have great significance. The generality of poverty made the city dweller and the farmer, the southerner and the northerner, more alike than different. In
present-day America the critical point is that the poor are different in
ways other than their not having money. Nor are the crucial differences particularized in the individual or attitudinal; they are all-pervasive
and embrace each of the groups which are poor. The differences are
lodged deep in the marrow of existence, with a high incidence of chronic
disease, mental illness, low education, and long-term unemployment
characterizing the poor.

Thus, being poor—at least for families in 1960—may mean being
non-white, living in a rural farm area, having a large number of children, or having as head of the family a non-earner, a female, or a person either over 65 or between the ages of 14 and 24. It may—and often
does—mean that one belongs to a disadvantaged, discriminated-against
group. To say that being poor means, say, being non-white makes pov-

erty as an idea more rather than less complicated; the policy correlatives more fearful. How can one make the non-white white, the aged non-aged? The problem seems to escape solution, to be disembodied from the economy and from the growth and development processes usually thought of as affecting income flows which, at least in the more traditional approach, could fill the gap of unsatisfied needs.

Pi Coefficients

If the risk of poverty has for some groups been high, how has this risk been affected by the workings of the economy? To find an answer to this question, the relative attachment to low income of people with different poverty-linked characteristics has to be measured for a series of years.

In this study the New School staff developed a measure of the association between a population's possession of a given characteristic and an income below specified levels. Such a measure was found in the small modification of a relatively simple statistical technique, the Pi coefficient. The degree of attachment so measured gives a numerical value which represents the strength of the association between the possession of the characteristics and incomes both below and above given levels. A value of +1 in such a coefficient means a perfect association between low income and a given characteristic, and a value of -1 means that there is no association whatsoever. In applying the Pi coefficient test we used three levels of low income reflecting as closely as possible the poverty band discussed earlier. The dollar values in 1960 were $2,500, $4,500, and $5,500; but these dollar values varied from year to year, being adjusted as far as feasible to changes in the price level. For simplicity we shall therefore refer to the income levels as "very low," "middle low," and "high low." The value of the Pi coefficient is neither a measure of incidence nor of composition. It is rather a net, unaffected by changes in the make-up of the various groups; without saying anything about the causal nexus between low income and a given characteristic, it measures the risk of low income. It permits, through the use of constant dollars, year-to-year comparisons for a given characteristic and among characteristics. The data so obtained provide the rough equivalent of actuarial tables. Risk here is thus the risk of which Frank Knight speaks in Risk, Uncertainty, and Profit and is akin to the Weberian notion of the "life chances."

The Pi coefficient test was applied for each year from the end of World War II to 1960 and for all characteristics for which data were available. The computations are explained and the resulting data are available in Appendix 8.

The degree of association of the various characteristics with low income, by this measure, was in general consistent with what one would expect from the results of the other tests of association just reported. The characteristics for which the Pi coefficients were calculated can be broadly ranked in decreasing order of strength of association with low income in 1960 as follows:

Families	Unattached Individuals
Head a non-earner	Non-earner
Head 65 or over	Age 65 or over
Rural farm	Rural Farm
Female head	Female
Non-white	Non-white
Head 14-24 years of age	14-24 years of age
Six or more children under 18 years of age	

It will be seen that the broad ranking is the same for families and unattached individuals. This is the general pattern. There are some variations from one low-income level to another, the principal one being that families headed by a person 65 or over showed markedly less association with the "very low" income level in 1960 than with the "middle low" or the "high low" level.

Over the thirteen-year period 1947-1960, these characteristics tended to become more closely associated with low income. For families, an increase of association was observed for most of these characteristics, and for two of the characteristics—rural farm and female head—the increase appeared at each of the three income levels. For non-white families and families with six or more children under 18, however, the association weakened at all three income levels. For the unattached, a more definite pattern of increase of association was found, and it held more generally for all income levels.

Another general finding from this study of Pi coefficients was that the risk of poverty remained relatively untouched by the ups and downs of the economy during the period surveyed. Neither the 1948-49 recession, the second postwar recession of 1952-54, nor the 1958 recession materially affected the risk; nor did the upswings in the other years. For those living at low levels of income, in other words, business expansion did not significantly reduce the risk of poverty nor did business contractions increase it very much.

Characteristic by characteristic, the calculations of the Pi coefficients tell the following.

Non-earner.   In spite of the existence of various schemes of unemployment, extended unemployment, and welfare payments, and other
possible sources of income such as help from relatives, families
headed by a non-earner are obviously exposed to a very high risk of
being poor. The Pi coefficients were high for such families and also
for individual non-earners at each of the three levels of low income.
Understandably, no other characteristic was as clearly tied to low income. But the link was closer for families than for unattached individuals.

An important finding is that the attachment of these unemployed
groups to poverty tended to become stronger year after year, regardless of the state of the economy. For the unemployed, it seems, there
is no boom and recession but only depression.

Non-white.   The poverty of the non-white is very special. The
measure of attachment devised here—and census numbers are not
color-biased—underlines the strength of the relationship of non-whites
to low income. After 1954, except at the highest of the three income
levels, the Pi coefficients also indicate that there was a tightening of
the relationship—an increase in the risk of poverty—as the decade
progressed. The general improvement in business conditions which
took place between 1954 and 1957 was not greatly felt by non-white
families with incomes below $1,500 and $2,500 (and their adjusted
equivalents). Nor did they feel the improvement following the 1958
recession.

For the non-white families at the $3,500 level (and its equivalents)
the situation is quite different. At this level it can be seen that non-
white families, in a manner of speaking, step above poverty during
periods of expansion, only to be pushed back down by the forces that
make for business contraction. This may be because families at these
income levels are more likely to have at least some members with industrial experience. Those at the lower levels, it may be surmised,
have many unemployed and family members with income from sources
(service employment, public assistance) which are less sensitive to
the ups and downs of the business cycle or to secular expansion.

Because unattached individuals as a group have lower incomes,
non-whiteness is less of a liability for them than for families. As
with the unattached non-earner, the situation of the very poor unattached non-white has worsened with time and has been related to the
business cycle. On the other hand, in 1959 and 1960 the Pi coefficients for unattached non-whites moved up noticeably, whereas those

for unattached non-earners went down, suggesting that in a period of
weak economic recovery, non-whites fare less well than other unattached persons.

We shall have more to say about the association between non-
whiteness and poverty in a later section.

Age 65 or over.   There is, in the value of the Pi coefficients, evidence that, from 1947 to 1960—probably mostly because of Social Security—families headed by a person 65 or over moved up the income
scale, but not out of the poverty range. That is, by 1960 an aged head
exposed the family to less risk of being in the "very low" income category but more risk of being in either of our other two income categories.

Unattached individuals aged 65 or over are condemned to obliv-
ion by the obscurity of the statistics as well as by the feebleness
of age; there is a hint that they are better off than families headed by
persons of similar age but that their incomes are less sensitive to improvements in the business cycle. The ameliorative effects of the Social Security program are not manifest among the unattached. One possible explanation is that there are a disproportionate number of females
among older single individuals, many of whom may not qualify for old-
age and survivors' benefits under the federal program, since their
participation in covered employment is, and has been, considerably
below the male rate.

Rural farm residence.   The risk of poverty in the rural farm group
has recently increased no matter how looked at. This poverty-linked
group is numerically less important today than in 1947. The association of the now smaller farm population with low income, however,
has become considerably stronger. An additional finding—not unex-
pected—is that the association appears closely related to the economy's cyclical path. In the 1948-49 recession, for example, the association became much stronger at all levels of low income. It weakened
somewhat following the recession; between 1952 and 1954 a significant
tightening of the relationship, paralleling the second postwar recession, took place. After the second recession the values of the Pi coefficients at the lowest income level and the middle level no longer
paralleled the movements of the general economy. This would indicate, through 1957, a greater association to poverty than in the earlier period. At the highest of the low-income points the coefficients
have remained more clearly related to general business conditions,

especially after 1955. The coefficients gradually weakened through 1958, increased in 1959, and moved down again in 1960.

Although there is some indication that the association with low income has increased for unattached individuals in the rural farm category, the trend lacks the strength found for families. In general the coefficients were of a smaller magnitude, and although cyclical influences can be found, again the parallel is weaker than in the case of families. At the lowest level of income, exclusion of the 1947 coefficient would leave little in the way of a secular trend. The impact of the 1948 and 1958 recessions is evident but the 1953 downturn left no impression on the coefficient.

A later section will go into the subject of rural farm poverty in more detail.

Female.   The statistical classification "female, head of household" is a colorless way of saying that death, disease, divorce, or desertion has claimed the husband and devastated normal family life. Here a woman holds together the family remnants; a synthesis of mother, father, housewife, and breadwinner, she is too poor to be fully any of them and as a breadwinner she mostly fails. The risk of poverty for a family headed by a female is high, and apparently growing, as the sharp increases in the Pi coefficients reveal a well-pronounced and clear trend.

Changes in the situation of families headed by women, where no man is present, as represented in our measure conflict sharply with changes in the general state of business conditions. In this case the coefficients may be more a reflection of the changes taking place in the non-poverty-linked group than in the poverty-linked population. An over-all strong association with poverty certainly existed at the beginning of the period covered and it grew over time. The increase in the risk of poverty for female heads of families was most apparent when the rest of the population was relatively prosperous. The worsening condition of these families appeared to be arrested only in the years when the nation suffered serious economic setbacks. This state of affairs, which is reflected in the values of the Pi coefficients, has created the impression that women heads of families improved their condition countercyclically. Obviously not so. Changes in the coefficients can be a reflection of either a change in the status of our poverty-linked population or a change in the conditions of the remaining population.

The correlation between poverty and single females is not as close as that where a family is involved. Unattached females are, besides

the young living alone and often doing well, the lone widows or divor-
cees, the spinsters, the dutiful daughters whose presence has all but
been forgotten by an America continually glorifying married life. Their
condition is not comparable with that of the female head of household,
nor has their risk of being poor increased. This is to be expected,
for single females suffer from only one economic disadvantage, their
sex, while female heads of families face a complex of problems. There
is here no clear relation between changes in the value of the coefficients
measuring attachment to poverty and post-World War II business fluctuations. A factor blurring the relationship is the composition of this
group, which contains many elderly women no longer in the labor force,
living on pensions, welfare or gifts—income sources immune to changes
in business conditions.

The large and young families.   Increase in family size in recent
years does not seem to have affected the poor population very significantly; family size is scattered fairly evenly among consumer units at
all income levels.

Among low-income families, the proportion with four, five, and
six persons, as Lampman noted, has fallen drastically.[1] Yet in the
present study, when need levels for families of different size were adjusted, it was found that in 1960 a large proportion (36 per cent) of
families with income below the "minimum subsistence" level were
families of seven or more, and that this proportion had been smaller
(24 per cent) in 1949.[2]

Size of family, when there are two adults with varying numbers of
children under 18, can also be statistically related to poverty. Families with two children under 18 tend to be relatively well off, but those
with six or more tend to be poor. The coefficients of association for
families with two children under 18 were found in our study to fluctu-
ate narrowly around -.2500; those with six or more than six, around
+.2500.

Very young families—with the family head between 14 and 24—
made up a slightly smaller segment of the total population in 1950 than

1. Robert J. Lampman, The Low Income Population and Economic Growth,
Study Paper No. 12, Joint Economic Committee, 86th Cong., 1st sess.,
December 1959.

2. These figures are not entirely comparable to others reported in earlier
pages relating to the count of the poor, which were based on family personal income. For lack of data on personal income by family size, money income was
used in the present instance. The "minimum subsistence" need level in 1960 for
a family of 3.7 persons was, as indicated in Appendix 5, $2,554.

in 1947; but, as observed earlier, their incidence in the low-income population has increased. At this age level, it is seen, the honor of being "family head" often brings with it today, and particularly since 1957, more risk of poverty. The increase in the risk of poverty for the very young family, traceable in the tables in Appendix 8, depends— as is the case with other characteristics—on where in the range of low income measurement is taken: the increase is greatest at the lowest of our three income levels and less at the middle level. At the topmost level there was also some increase after 1948.

Nowhere, as far as the very young family is concerned, are either the values of the Pi coefficient very high or the evidence of the poverty cut-off level very significant. Indeed, the poverty of the young is part of the life cycle. For part of this group, poverty is only a temporary condition, as college or other training will make later affluence almost a certainty. For most others, however, low income is no momentary detour; it foreshadows a life of poverty. And the situation of very young families is worsening. The situation of the young in contemporary America typifies the situation of the poor: submerged.

The Non-Poverty-Linked Population

A check on the validity of the approach used in this study is provided by repeating the analysis for a population without the characteristics that have been examined. This was done for families headed by a white male aged 25-34, and with two children under 18. The data showed that in 1960 this combination of attributes was much less frequent in the low income brackets and much more prevalent in the high income brackets. Individuals with these characteristics appeared in 1960 not to have a high risk of poverty. Twelve years earlier, in 1948, their risk of being poor was almost twice as great, even by 1948 standards.

On the other hand, the previously described constellation of poverty-linked characteristics was more evident in low income brackets in 1960 than in the late 1940's. The greater concentration of the population with poverty-linked characteristics at low-income levels in 1960 appears due to the fact that the population groups whose relative income level rose between the late 1940's and 1960 were predominantly those without poverty-linked characteristics.

The Risk of Poverty in the Affluent Society

Our study emphasizes the fact that in the 1960's the poor are underprivileged. "Underprivileged" has long been a fashionable word, as it seemed to offend less than the crasser one "poor." On the whole, until the period discussed herein, it was an inappropriate designation. Now it fits.

The poverty of the affluent society is the poverty of those clearly out of the mainstream of American life. The underprivileged are in, but not of, the market society. They sit outside, neither buyers nor sellers, discriminated against socially and economically. Their poverty is the result of special circumstances, rather than of the rate, or of the changes in the rate, of economic activity. They are not part of the prevailing economic structure.

The discovery that "income classes are not purely economic classes, but must be defined at the lower end, ... in terms of special situations and racial discrimination"[1] is the leitmotif of recent work on this topic. Gunnar Myrdal in his Challenge to Affluence points to the same theme and phenomenon when he notes that America has developed an underclass.

From this recognition of the structural nature of poverty we carry the argument further into the implications for policy. Policies aimed at the economic development of the total society and believed, therefore, to help the poor are of very limited use in the fight against poverty. From the fact that poverty is a structural problem follows the requirements that policy action be structurally oriented. It won't do to argue—as Keyserling and Harrington do—that poverty will be done away with by policies aimed at bringing about full employment, though these are prerequisites and have a social and economic value and priority of their own. The substantial reduction of poverty calls for measures pinpointed to those particular social and structural characteristics of the affluent society that have created a large pool of underprivileged.

1. Henry Pachter, "The Income Revolution," Dissent, Summer 1957, p. 316.

5

The convergence of
poverty-linked characteristics

IT IS most important to note that many individuals will have more
than one of the characteristics we have found to be linked to low income.
The risk of poverty is significantly greater among persons affected by
a congruence of traits than by only one poverty-linked trait.

Analysis of 1960 census data allowed a count of low-income family
units that had one or more of four key characteristics—non-white,
family head 65 years of age or over, female family head, and rural
farm residence. Using the three income levels that approximate the
reference points in the discussion of the poverty band—"minimum subsistence" ($2,500 or less for a four-member family in 1960); "mini-
mum adequacy" ($4,500); and "minimum comfort" ($5,500)—the New
School poverty study staff organized data on the number of families
having these four characteristics either separately or in any combination. This was done simply by adding or subtracting census figures
on the number of families with the indicated characteristics at each
income level. Since there was no double counting in these figures,
those families with, say, two characteristics, instead of only one,
form a separate and additional increment.

About a third of all families in the United States in 1960 had one
or more of these characteristics. Thus, aged families, Negro families, broken families, and farm families—or families with varying
combinations of these characteristics—were a minority of the nation's
population. However, as Appendix 10 shows, such families accounted
in 1960 for the bulk of the poor. Seven out of ten families with income
below the "subsistence" level were of these types; six out of ten families with income below the "adequacy" level; and almost half of families whose income was below the "comfort" level.

Of the characteristics examined, that of age was the most promi-
nent. Under the four single-attribute groupings, aged heads of families led the list below all three income levels (Appendix 11). They
were followed, in descending order, by families headed by a female,

non-white families, and rural farm families. If the characteristics
are taken not only singly but in all their combinations, the same se-
quence is found.

When a family has not merely one but two or more of these characteristics, the probability of poverty is generally increased, and
sometimes becomes overwhelming. The study revealed (Appendix 10)
that for all but one of the six subgroups with two attributes the proportion below the "subsistence" level in 1960 was better than half:

Family Head	No. of Families	Per Cent Below "Subsistence"
Rural farm, non-white	208,047	78.3
Female, non-white	743,115	64.6
Aged, non-white	331,316	62.6
Aged, rural farm	489,732	54.9
Female, rural farm	73,842	54.8
Aged, female	787,975	37.2

For these twice-disadvantaged groups the chances of having income in
1960 below the "adequacy" level were approximately 75 per cent or
better, again with the exception of families headed by an aged female.
The chances of being below the "comfort" level were more than eight
in ten for all but the one group just named. Since the statistics deal
only with the number and not the size of families, the degree of poverty within the individual families would also vary.

What was found true for the congruence of these four characteristics can be generalized for others. One can assume, for instance, that
bad housing, inadequate education, or poor health are probably unseen
added factors in many instances. With presently available data, it
cannot be determined exactly how many of the 20 million abject poor
in 1960 were disadvantaged because of poor health, mental disease,
poor housing, or inadequate education. By a very rough estimate,
which can be off as much as 50 per cent, we judge that of these 20 million, more than two-thirds, or somewhere between 12 and 14 million,
were deficient in health, either mental or physical, or in education,
and very probably in both.

To pursue the implications of the convergence of characteristics,
the poverty study staff developed a model for two characteristics—poor
health and subnormal education—each of which appears to affect individuals with a different risk of poverty. This is described in Appendix 9. The model, based on a hypothetical joint frequency distribution,
suggests that with the assumed distributions of characteristics the risk
of poverty is at its greatest for relatively small numbers of people.

But it also underlines how the poverty-linked characteristics have effects proportionate to their intensity. Thus, an individual's education
can be more or less substandard depending on whether he has completed, say, zero, 6, or 9 years of education. One may be more or
less mentally disturbed; more or less unemployed; and so on. Truly,
a woman cannot be more or less head of household—she either is or is
not—yet the intensity of the characteristic "woman head of household"
depends on whether the woman is the sole provider for 1, 3, 5, or 6
children and on whether she does or does not have relatives to help her.
For the characteristic "non-white" a continuum cannot easily be established, yet here too there are in fact socio-economic gradations reflecting different degrees of skin pigmentation.

The model used in our analysis refers to a situation at one point
in time. Yet it is recognized that certain conditions change over time.[1]
In this study, it was not possible to probe in depth the extent to which
the abject poor form a pool with given rates of "inflow" and "outflow."
The data used in the Pi coefficients, for example, have shown how
closely certain demographic characteristics remain attached to low
levels of income. They tell nothing about whether the poor groups are
made up of the same families or people year after year or from one
generation to the next. That poverty involves a significant long-term
relationship which goes beyond the workings of the economy has been
suggested. Common sense and observation imply that the conditions
that lead to poverty make themselves felt over time—else what would
result might be an emergency situation, not a long-term condition.
The heuristic model presented in Appendix 9 suggests the first step in
the dynamics of poverty. It is hoped that it will help open a way to the
study of how poverty reproduces itself from generation to generation.

1. English investigators of poverty in the 1920's hypothesized about the life
cycle of a typical English male living all his life in or barely above poverty. The
hypothetical impoverished English worker of the 1920's, they posited, begins his
life in infant and juvenile dependency, and sinks below the "poverty line" before
age 14, when he becomes a wage earner. In his early twenties, before acquiring
a wife and children, he lives above the line. In his thirties, when his children become a burden, he and his family fall below the line. This hypothesis combines
the traditional concept of the single "poverty line" and the concept that duration
through time is an essential dimension of poverty. It emphasizes the fact that
poverty has its most distressing effects on children who have not yet reached employment age and on women in the child-bearing years. See Arthur L. Bowley
and Margaret H. Hogg, Has Poverty Diminished?, London School of Economics
and Political Science, Studies in Economics and Political Science No. 82, London,
P. S. King and Sons, 1925.

The geography of low income

POVERTY, without a doubt, has a geographic dimension. Employment opportunities are not equally distributed. Their specific availability reflects the history and ecology of industrialization and economic growth. The lower East Side in New York City is a "poor" area. So are the many counties certified as development areas by the Area Redevelopment Administration of the federal government. Those living in Appalachia and certain parts of the South have a very great risk of being poor.

The true significance of one's residence may be that it coincides with an area either of labor surplus or of labor shortage. It may place one in an area where structural changes in the economy have brought about job obsolescence or rapidly expanding job opportunity. In these terms, we are dealing with changes in the labor market, which will be the subject of a later section. Here only the statistical relationship between poverty and place of residence will be discussed.

Relative Urban Advantage

Foremost among the myths about poverty is that it is predominantly rural. Indeed, in rural farm areas, a larger proportion of the population is plagued by low income. But traditional life on the farm is fast disappearing. By the time John F. Kennedy took office, the agricultural population had declined to less than 8 per cent of the total. The urban base is so much larger that the sheer magnitude of urban poverty overshadows its agrarian counterpart.

The chief gravitational pull the city exerts on the farm is economic opportunity. The bait is a job, the wages it pays and even more the hope it offers. Many people in U. S. cities are poor. But the risk of being poor in the city is less than in the country. Some city incomes are low, but in general city incomes are not as low as rural farm incomes. This is "relative urban advantage."

Appendix 13 analyzes the relative distribution of the low-income population in urban, rural farm, and rural non-farm areas in 1949 and 1958 at three different levels of income. From this we find: (1) Well over half of the families with income below $1,000 in 1949 lived outside urban areas and were either rural farm or rural non-farm. The same situation held in 1958 for families in an income category (below $1,500) approximately equivalent in purchasing power. (2) In the next higher category of income ($2,000 per year in 1949 and $2,500 in 1958), again more than half of the families were rural residents. (3) But in the third income class ($3,500 per year in 1949 and $4,500 for 1958), a clear numerical majority of the families lived in the cities. To this we must add the fact that more of the unattached in each low income class were in cities in these two years. Thus, in terms of numbers in both years, the majority of those classifiable as poor lived in cities.

A smaller percentage of city than of rural families were poor, however. Take the year 1958, for instance. In that year, 6.7 per cent of urban families under $1,500 income contrasted with 27.1 per cent of rural farm and 8.5 per cent of rural non-farm families. Similar relationships obtained in the other categories of low income. While more poor families live in cities, city families have less chance of being poor. For the unattached individual this is even clearer. The chance of the "loner" being poor in the city is much less than in the hinterlands.

Size of Urban Community

The employment opportunities of town and metropolis differ also. Large metropolitan centers usually contain a wider range of industries and occupations. Loss of a job in a large city is not necessarily as catastrophic as in a small town.

In very large cities the fall in the incidence of poverty is as clear as is the rise in median income. (See Appendix 12.) Cities of a million or more show a substantially lower incidence of poverty than cities of 250,000 to one million: the decrease is more marked here than between communities in smaller size classes in Appendix 12. Median income, for both families and individuals, is also higher in the largest cities than in the smallest towns. Its steady fall with decreasing size of community is broken only by the unexpectedly higher incomes of individuals in cities of 25,000 to 50,000 than in cities of up to a million inhabitants.

The data in Appendix 12 picture the extent of small-town poverty for "the loners." In communities of 2,500 to 25,000 in 1960, nearly two out of every five unattached persons had incomes under $1,000 and about three-quarters received less than $3,000 per year.

Regional Disadvantage—The South

In spite of the fact that national forces clearly are dominant, regional economic differentials have been found to persist throughout the United States. Average levels of income vary from one part of the country to another; states and regions differ in size and rate of growth of population, employment and economic activity. For most indicators, the differential history of economic growth is sufficient explanation. Regional economic analysis has focused attention on the South.

That the South is poor has long been known. In a report prepared in 1938 by the National Emergency Council, the South—an underdeveloped area within the most developed country in the world—was labeled "the nation's economic problem No. 1." The Council's report recognized that much of southern poverty was the poverty of the social infrastructure—inadequate schooling and limited public services, meager facilities for research which might lead to technological development and a population not as richly endowed as in the rest of the nation.

Since 1938 economic growth—"brought about not by the unseen hand of economic forces but by the long arm of national policy"[1]—has helped the integration of the South into the American economy. The South is now a growing economy; it shares in the national efforts of "want creation" of the affluent society. Indeed, the growth rate of the South—since 1929—is higher than that of any other national region. Yet a century after the Civil War, poverty remains deeply ingrained in southern life. Whether measured by low income or by high functional illiteracy, by the quality of its housing or by the health of its people, the South lags behind the rest of the nation. It drags low income across one-third of the states. Within a "core" of seven southern states low income actually embraces a majority of the population.

One needs to define the term "South." In this study, two definitions were used, one the Census Bureau's definition and the other, a subgroup of "core" states. The following states are included in the Census definition: Alabama, Arkansas, Delaware, Florida, Georgia, Kentucky, Louisiana, Mississippi, Maryland, North Carolina, Oklahoma, South Carolina, Tennessee, Virginia, West Virginia, and the District of Columbia. Core states—referred to in our tables as "core-South"—include Mississippi, Arkansas, North and South Carolina, Alabama, Tennessee, and Kentucky. A first consideration leading to selection of these particular seven states was the fact that these states had roughly the highest proportions of families under our low-income

1. A. Goldschmidt, "The Development of the U.S. South" in *Scientific American*, September 1963, p. 229.

points in 1960. The second consideration was that the core group
showed less progress in reducing the low-income population during the
1950's than most other southern states.

Looking first at the broader, U. S. Census definition of the South,
one concludes from the low-income data (Appendix 14) that there is a
decided disadvantage associated with southern residence. Of the total
number of families living in the southern region, slightly over 21 per
cent had incomes below $2,000 in 1960. The comparable percentage
for the United States was 13. The gap was somewhat narrower in the
next two income classes. About a third of all southern family units
had money incomes below $3,000 while only slightly more than a fifth
of all U. S. families (which, of course, include southern families) were
below this level. Under $4,000, the southern proportion approached
45 per cent, while the figure for the United States as a whole was 31
per cent.

Unattached individuals living in the South, too, are, on the basis
of 1960 figures, more liable to be poor. The rate of poverty in 1960
was about twice as high for southern individuals as for southern families, except at the upper income limits used in the present analysis.
An individual southerner in 1960 ran a greater risk of being poverty-
stricken than the average unrelated individual in the country as a
whole. However, the distance separating the two was not as great as
that separating families in the two categories.

Any comparison of southern income with the national average
brings inevitable warnings that the racial and rural character of the
region frustrates simple generalizations. Rural areas are poor and
the South is the most rural area of the country. Negroes are poor and
the South still has a higher proportion of Negroes than other regions.
These factors can, however, be eliminated from the statistics. Appendix 14 supplies the necessary data for this analysis as well. Here
the percentages of total, white, urban, and white urban families
throughout the country with incomes under $2,000, $3,000, and $4,000
in 1960 are compared with their counterparts in the South and in the
core area.

Comparing, for example, the proportion of all families and of
southern families with 1960 incomes under $2,000, the proportion is
found to be greater by 63 per cent in the South and by 109 per cent in
the core states. Similar calculations for white families only yield a
figure of 52 per cent for the South and 89 per cent for the core group.
Comparing urban families only, the results are 53 per cent and 81 per
cent. When both race and residence variables are held constant and
one deals only with comparisons of white urban families, the percentages are 35 and 40 respectively. The net effect of holding race and

the urban-rural factor constant is to cut the difference between the nation as a whole and the South from 63 to 35 per cent; that is, a little over two-fifths of the difference is washed out. For the core states, roughly three-fifths of the difference disappears. In the "core-South," holding the urban-rural factor constant is even more revealing than in the South as defined by the Census Bureau. In these core states, the poorest non-whites obviously are rural residents. But differences between the general population and the "core-South" still remain, even in the white urban group. It is interesting to see that the relative advantage of white urban families over all families in the "core-South" is greater than in the whole South. It is perhaps an American parallel, in our area of underdevelopment, to the off-cited polarization of rich and poor in underdeveloped countries.

The pattern for unattached individuals follows the general pattern of family income, except that so many unattached are poor that the advantage of a white skin or a city address does not help as much.

We have been talking of geographic factors. But the cause of poverty in an area is rarely location alone. The cause is that such areas have a higher proportion of their population with poverty-linked characteristics. The various studies on the population characteristics of depressed areas prepared for the Area Redevelopment Administration, and the New School poverty study staff's work on employment (which will be reported on in a later section), all stress the differential population characteristics—especially as far as age and education are concerned—of the depressed areas. Thus, any isolated locational notion of poverty is of limited use for policy. The phrase that Galbraith popularized, "pockets of poverty," is helpful as it locates the area of action; but it tells us little about the action to be taken.

7

Poverty among negroes

IT WILL by now be apparent that poverty among Negroes—or non-whites[1]—is a thread running through this entire report. Indeed, the sole fact of non-whiteness was found to be poverty-linked. For this reason, and because so much has been written on the subject since the New School study began, this section need only call attention to some of our main findings.

Three conclusions emerged from the New School study's examination of the economic position of non-whites: (1) in the years since World War II, the economic gains of the non-white population have been less than proportional to those of whites; (2) the gainers in the non-white group itself are in a minority; and (3) the relative position of a significant majority of non-whites has worsened.

While full employment and a rising trend of incomes for all are effective in lessening the impact of discrimination, such conditions are in themselves not sufficient to solve the economic and social problems of Negroes. Indications of improvement are not difficult to find. Their median wage and salary income, in real terms, i.e., in constant dollars, was higher in 1960 than in 1940. The proportion owning their homes grew. Their housing improved. Negroes were somewhat better represented in skilled and semiskilled jobs in 1960. The proportion of Negro men in white-collar occupations was larger than it had been in 1940. By 1962, 17 per cent of the non-whites in the labor force were in white-collar occupations.[2]

In 1960, however, when less than one out of every ten families in the nation was non-white, families that were non-white still accounted for one out of every five families with income below $500 (Appendix 6).

1. In this section "non-white" and "Negro" are used as interchangeable terms. The key data are for non-whites. Of the 20.5 million non-whites in 1960, according to the Bureau of the Census, 92 per cent (18.9 million) were Negroes.

2. See, for example, U.S. Department of Labor, The Economic Situation of Negroes in the United States, Bulletin S-3, October 1960; and Matthew A. Kessler, "Economic Status of Non-white Workers," Monthly Labor Review, July 1963.

Further evidence that the economic status of Negroes still lags, and is essentially different from that of whites who are poor, is provided by a special tabulation of 1960 census data, in Appendix 15.

As the table in Appendix 15 makes clear, strongly marked differences are found in the proportions of white and non-white families at each level of low income. This proves true even with the exclusion, either in whole or in part, of factors positively associated with low income such as regional location, rural residence, unemployment, female head of family, or advanced age. Eliminating the South reduces the proportions of families at low income levels for both whites and non whites. But it does not fundamentally affect the pattern of poverty as a distinctive function of color. The proportion of four-person families with incomes under $4,000 in 1960 was about three times as large for the non-whites as for the white group in the United States as a whole.

Of all the urban non-white four-person families in the United States in 1960, almost one out of ten fell into the less than $2,000 income class, and better than two out of five into the less than $4,000 class. In the case of white families, the ratios for these classes were not quite one out of fifty and slightly more than one out of ten. When the South is excluded, non-white urban families remain far more heavily represented than white in the low-income population.

Historical differences between Negroes and whites in school enrollment, completion of elementary and secondary school, college attendance and graduation have all recently been reduced. Improvement in the educational status of Negroes in recent decades is manifested by the sharp increase in the years of schooling attained by the average young adult. By 1962, the discrepancy in the median number of years of school completed between non-white and white men aged 25 to 29 had been reduced to 1.3 years.[1] Today, with probably less than 5 per cent of the Negro population unable to read or write, illiteracy has for practical purposes been eradicated except in the older age groups. Of non-whites between the ages of 14 and 22, probably one per cent are illiterate; of those 65 and older, about 25 per cent. (Among whites, the percentages for these two age groups are about half of one per cent and less than 5 per cent.)[2]

Quantitative measures of educational progress among Negroes are impressive. But qualitatively speaking the Negro population remains

1. Kessler, loc. cit., p. 193.

2. The Economic Situation of Negroes in the United States, p. 35; Marion Hayes, "A Century of Change: Negroes in the U.S. Economy, 1860-1960," Monthly Labor Review, December 1962, p. 1361; Statistical Abstract of the United States, 1963, p. 123.

educationally disadvantaged. The Negro youth encounters poorly prepared teachers and outmoded curricula. He has less access to trained
counselors and guidance. He attends more crowded schools, and has
less use of new equipment and textbooks. If he graduates from high
school he is less well prepared for college. He is more likely to go to
a low ranking college.[1]

In addition to the qualitative inferiority of their education, a significant finding of the New School study was that the educational process
of Negroes is not proportionately reflected in their income position.
Given the same number of years of schooling, Negroes can almost in-
variably be found employed in lower paying, less skilled occupations.
Within the same occupational group, non-whites are customarily paid
less than whites, particularly where the educational levels of both are
higher than the national average. For unskilled and semiskilled workers of low education the differential is less.[2] While education remains
an important determinant of the kind of work a man is qualified to do,
race in itself, as has been shown, imposes modifications of the probability of his employment in the highest possible category and the earnings he receives.

Non-white women are handicapped in their employment in very
much the same way as non-white men. Ten per cent of the non-white
women working in 1959 were employed as domestics as compared to
one per cent of the white women in the labor force. For more skilled,
better paying jobs the ratio was reversed: only 12 per cent of working
non-white women were secretaries or clerks, compared to 44 per cent
of the white women who worked.[3]

1. See, for example, Henry S. Ashmore, The Negro and the Schools, Univer-
sity of North Carolina Press, Chapel Hill, 1954; Truman M. Pierce, James B.
Kincheloe, R. Edgar Moore, Galen N. Drewrey, and Bennie E. Carmichael,
White and Negro Schools in the South: An Analysis of Biracial Education, Pren-
tice-Hall, Englewood Cliffs, N.J., 1955; James B. Conant, Slums and Suburbs:
A Commentary on Schools in Metropolitan Areas, McGraw-Hill, New York, 1961;
A. Harry Passow, editor, Education in Depressed Areas, Bureau of Publications,
Teachers College, Columbia University, New York, 1963; Paul Woodring and
John Scanlon, editors, American Education Today, McGraw-Hill, New York,
1963, pp. 121-123.

2. White clerical workers had, in 1959, a mean income of $3,961, as com-
pared to $3,364 for non-whites. White craftsmen earned $4,148 and non-whites
$2,833. The difference was greatest among managers, proprietors, and offi-
cials, with whites earning $5,058 a year and non-whites $2,575. Daniel
Creamer, "Some Determinants of Low Family Income," Economic Development
and Cultural Change, April 1961, p. 437.

3. Arnold Katz, "Educational Attainment of Workers," Monthly Labor Review,
February 1960, p. 115.

8

Education

IT IS a simple statistical fact that low educational attainment is closely associated with low income. Available figures, for instance, reveal that every school year completed brings measurable dollar dividends. In 1959, unskilled workers had completed a median of 8.5 years of schooling; semiskilled workers, 10.0; craftsmen and foremen, 11.0; clerical workers, 12.5; professional and technical workers, 16.4 years. The educational and occupational differences had proportionately differing incomes. Thus, the median earnings for unskilled workers (excluding farm laborers) were $2,834; for semiskilled workers, $4,101; for craftsmen and foremen, $5,272; for clerical workers, $4,691; and for professional and technical workers, $6,287.[1]

The financial advantage of higher education is marked. An elementary school graduate could expect to receive in the course of his lifetime $52,000 more than one who did not complete the eighth grade and $76,000 less than a high school graduate. The college graduate, however, could earn an estimated $177,000 more than the high school graduate.[2]

Educational attainment, in years of school completed, also differentially affects frequency of employment, number of hours worked, and wage rates. This fact was determined by University of Michigan reseachers, who equated a sample of heads of spending units for age, marital status, number of minor children, physical condition, extent of local unemployment, race, differences in education between husband and wife, their attitude toward work, and financial situation and plans. When this was done, large differences in income remained, attributable solely to educational achievement. As the number of school years completed increased, both the probability of finding employment and the hourly wage rate were higher. The number of hours worked during a

1. U.S. Bureau of the Census, Current Population Reports, Series P-20, No. 99, February 1960, p. 60; No. 35, January 1961, p. 52.

2. Herman P. Miller, "Annual and Lifetime Income in Relation to Education: 1939-1959," American Economic Review, December 1960, pp. 962-86.

year increased also for each additional year of school completed up to
sixteen years of schooling. [1]

Dropping Out

Approximately 40 per cent of all those who started high school at
the beginning of the 1960's were dropping out before graduation. [2] The
dropout rate is consistently highest where poverty is most concentrated—among rural, non-white, and urban slum populations. The simple
relationship between income of parents and percentage of dropouts is
shown in a report by the Census Bureau based on data for 1959. At a
family income level of $9,000 and over, the percentage of dropouts
was 3.6; in the income class $8,000-$8,999 the percentage rose to 7.2;
and when family income was as low as $3,000-$4,999 the dropout rate
was 19.2 per cent. [3]

In theory, public education puts opportunity equally within the
reach of all children. Supposedly, it wipes out class differences, utilizing tax money contributed by those best able to pay for the benefit of
the children of rich and poor alike. This is the ideal, but not the fact.
The U.S. public school system operates as a selection mechanism, fit-
ting individuals into the molds society requires. [4] Behind the often des-
perate efforts to maintain the appearance of equality of opportunity in
school and beyond it, a relentless competition goes on. For this competition the children of the poor are ill-fitted. By the time they have
entered school, children from culturally deprived homes are already
at a disadvantage. Their parents themselves have often suffered from
low educational attainment. Inadequate education is part of the life
style of the poor. This shows up early in poor reading skill. The pu-
pil who has trouble reading seldom catches up. Parents, children,

1. Martin David et al., Educational Achievement: Its Causes and Effects,
University of Michigan, Survey Research Center, Ann Arbor, 1961, p. 122.

2. "School Dropouts," National Education Association Research Memo, August 1961, p. 2.

3. U.S. Bureau of the Census, Current Population Reports, Series P-20, No.
110, 1960, p. 15.

4 John W. Gardner, Excellence: Can We Be Equal and Excellent Too?,
Harper & Row, New York, 1961, Chapter 7, "Education as a Sorting Out
Process."

and teachers alike may take it for granted that he never will do so. Extreme motivation is required for a child from such a background to lift himself to a higher level.

The disastrous occupational effects of dropping out are immediately apparent. A study of the first year's work experience of dropouts compared with that of high school graduates, for 1959, revealed that:

(1) While the majority in both groups began by doing unskilled work, 44 per cent of the high school graduates versus only 33 per cent of the dropouts progressed to skilled and semiskilled employment.

(2) Five times more dropouts than graduates were earning under $40 a week (or $2,000 a year), and three times more were getting $40 to $49 a week. Of those earning over $80 a week two-thirds had finished high school.

(3) It took most dropouts about ten weeks or more to find employment. Most graduates found jobs within three weeks of finishing school.

(4) After the first job, the unemployment rate for dropouts ranged from 10 per cent to 27 per cent as compared to a range of 3 per cent to 9 per cent for graduates. Dropouts were also unemployed for longer periods of time per year.[1]

Most students are said to leave school to "go to work" or because of "lack of interest." However, recent dropout investigations tell us that much more is involved. A Connecticut State study of dropouts compared the reason given for the dropout in the school record with those given by the student and the student's parents. The analysis, summarized in the accompanying table, is useful also because it distinguishes Negro and white students. The reasons noted most frequently in school records are "16 years old" and "work." The reasons given by both students and parents place considerably more weight on indifferent or discouraged student attitudes toward school. "Financial" reasons were given approximately the same weight by both pupils and parents. There was, however, a race differential: although Negro families as a group have significantly lower income than white families, fewer Negro students and their families stated that their motivation was lack of money. Evidently "pressure" on the whites was partly subjective.

The dynamic that eventually leads to dropping out is unclear. It is known that it begins early. If a child doesn't learn to read in the early grades, he runs a greater likelihood of dropping out later. Three times as many poor as good readers drop out of school and 80 per cent of the good readers, as compared to 45 per cent of the poor readers, graduate

1. David et al., op. cit., pp. 8-10.

2. Ruth Penty, Reading Ability and High School Dropouts, Bureau of Publications, Teachers College, Columbia University, 1956.

TABLE   2   Reasons Given for Leaving High School   (Per Cent)

Reason Stated	By School White Pupils	By School Negro Pupils	By Pupil White Pupils	By Pupil Negro Pupils	By Parent White Pupils	By Parent Negro Pupils
Lack of interest, disliked school, teachers, subjects; discouraged	8	5	47	41	39	34
Financial	--	--	23	16	22	18
Work	41	32	--	--	--	--
16 years old	32	24	--	--	--	--
Poor academic performance; failing	2	2	15	17	17	9
Asked to leave	8	13	6	3	2	1
Armed services	7	19	1	3	2	9
Don't know	--	--	5	16	8	14
Other	--	3	3	3	--	3

Source: Comparative Study of Negro and White Dropouts in Selected Connecticut High School, State of Connecticut, Commission on Civil Rights, Hartford, 1959, pp. 11-13.

Dropouts often are apathetic about trying to better themselves. A sample of dropouts, for instance, were questioned at the time of their leaving school and about a year later as to what attributes they thought made for success. The leading responses were "having the right training" and "brains," with "having the right training" given by over half the dropouts both before and after the first year of regular work experience. Despite this fact, even after the dropouts had had unsatisfactory work experience, no more than half regretted their decision to leave school. A sizable number said they would do the same thing again. [1]

The Effects of a Poor Environment

While the non-monetary aspects of low income are obviously important, the quality of being poor also needs consideration. The story

1. Marcia K. Freedman, "A Study of the Vocational Behavior of a Group of Academic School-leavers in Brooklyn," New York City Board of Education, 1962, unpublished, pp. 76 and 81. The sample was a favorably selected group of dropouts in that they had remained in school until age 16 or over, and had attended an academic high school.

here is so well known as hardly to require retelling: crowded housing, poor health, concentration of mental disorders—all contribute to limiting the educational attainments of the children of the poor.

Poor children generally have more and earlier responsibilities. Attendance in school is affected thereby. The poor child—particularly the boy—falls behind in school also because he is more frequently sick. Indeed, boys from families earning less than \$2,000—the abject poor— were in the later 1950's generally sick half again as often as those from families receiving between \$4,000 and \$6,000 per year.[1]

Schools attended by poor children are often overcrowded, under-staffed, and lacking in textbooks, remedial specialists, and countless other necessities. They are inadequate precisely where they need to be more than adequate.

Recognition and development of the potential of the young, too, is class-linked. Where middle and upper class parents think in terms of a college education for their offspring, lower class parents' aspirations usually stop at a high school diploma, at the very best. Poor parents, with little education, are more likely to believe in luck than in education and to be contemptuous of "book learning," in contrast to parents with more years of schooling, whose respect for education is often even greater than warranted. Indeed, among low-income families both the low educational attainments of the head of the household and the quality of family life create a social environment that leads the poor to believe that "education is not for them." The total family milieu, particularly for non-whites, encourages the rejection of formal schooling beyond the early years.

If the home environment of the poor tends to weaken the child's chance to escape poverty, the schools of the poor do not help either. If the school environment is to help introduce the child into the mainstream of American life and prepare him for participation and success in the labor market, it should provide him with an alternative to the self-defeating life of his family and his neighbors. This the slum school or the school of the depressed areas or the rural school of the South does not do. On the contrary, the school reinforces the surrounding environment. A child, no matter how ambitious and able, cannot learn much in schools with overcrowded classrooms in which most of the students are indifferent to learning, seriously disturbed, and frequently absent—schools whose older pupils have adopted the street gang as the substitute for home and family.

1. U.S. Department of Health, Education, and Welfare, Health Statistics, Disability Days, Series B-10, 1959, p. 29.

The Intergenerational Link

No one has ever asked about the level of education achieved by
Horatio Alger's father, but it has been proved over and over again that
the success of many a would-be Horatio Alger is indicated long before
his birth by his father's education. Earlier, as the history of a large
immigration of illiterates testifies, educational achievements did not
carry over so strongly from one generation to another. The family
life of the older immigrant group probably provided the children with
a different environment and a stronger motivation toward education.
In the 1950's and 1960's, it is important to remember too, educational
requirements are higher and the low-income populations are not made
up predominantly of immigrants.

Underscoring the impact of the father's education, the University
of Michigan Survey Research Center study found that education of the
father was the most powerful predictor of low income for the son even
after the data were corrected for mother's education, father's income
and occupation, number of siblings, religion, place of residence, sex,
age and race.[1] Having or not having money does not in and of itself
determine educational levels. The fact of low income does not pre-
clude the possibility of a high school or even a college diploma. The
level of education achieved by the father is more significant than his
income in determining the importance given to education in the home
and the degree of interest shown in the child's progress in school.
Disinterest is lethal.

Again, identifying the poor in other than income terms complicates
the analysis of poverty. It gives poverty another dimension of gloom.
There was a time when it could generally be assumed that individual
effort mattered, that human beings could control their future. It is no
longer clear that this can happen if individual efforts are not crowned
by a diploma. It is also clear that many of the poor, possibly believ-
ing that this means growing up absurd, are not getting and will not get
their diplomas. That if they do not get their diplomas they will stay
poor is certain.

1. David et al., op. cit., p. 14. See also David et al., Income and Welfare in
the U. S., McGraw-Hill, New York, 1962, pp. 371-83.

9

Housing

IN THE affluent society, housing statistics reflect a clear association with income. The intergenerational link of poverty appears forged in the syndrome bad education, bad housing, bad nutrition, limited knowledge of hygiene, late identification of disease. Housing, of course, is only part of the story. Good housing provides a favorable physical environment in which the human potential can be realized. But it does not teach children how to read, nor does it abolish discrimination or provide jobs; it does not cure the crippled or restore dead fathers; it may or may not entice back to the household a living but absent father.

The Link with Low Income

The housing components of the sample budgets for different years in Appendix 3, like the other components of these budgets, tell a story of gradual escalation of customary expenditure levels and currently accepted standards. Two indicators of adequacy in housing are in present general use, the number of persons per room and the physical condition of housing units. Appendix 16 indicates, paradoxically, that families and individuals in the $2,000-$2,999 and the $3,000-$3,999 income brackets were in 1960 relatively more overcrowded than those with less than $2,000 in income. This is largely because of the large numbers of unattached individuals and small families, especially aged, concentrated at the lowest income. Many aged stay on in the living quarters of their youth after their families decrease in size. Overcrowding in 1960 continued well above the $4,000 level. Families and unattached individuals above this level of income occupied more than half of the six million housing units with a person-per-room ratio over 1.01.[1]

The statistical connection between the condition of housing and income is more direct. In a nation known for its adoration of plumbing,

1. U.S. Census of Housing, 1960, Final Report.

68

for instance, lack of plumbing facilities, especially in urban areas, is a hallmark of American poverty. Three-fourths of all occupied housing units in 1960 were both sound and had all plumbing facilities; four-fifths were classed as being in sound condition (Appendix 17). But only about two-thirds of units occupied by those with incomes of less than $2,000 were sound, and just over half also had all plumbing facilities. Dilapidated housing was more than twice as frequent in this income bracket as in the total population.

Urban Slums, Rural Slums

Bad housing is not exclusively or even mainly urban, though public concern with city slums might suggest that it is. There is in fact more substandard housing outside than inside Standard Metropolitan Statistical Areas.[1]

There were 12.6 million occupied housing units in the United States in 1960 classifiable as substandard, about 6.9 million outside and 5.7 million inside SMSA's (Appendix 19). Of the 19 million occupied housing units outside SMSA's, only 12 million were in sound condition with complete plumbing facilities. Inside SMSA's about 28 million out of 34 million units were sound with all plumbing. Complete indoor plumbing facilities may be considered less necessary or indicative of poverty in rural areas; but the exclusion of this factor does not wipe out the difference between non-urban and urban housing. More occupied units outside than within SMSA's were substandard in 1960 quite apart from their status as to plumbing.

Poor housing also has a regional dimension that strengthens earlier findings about the poverty of the South. In spite of recent progress, the rate of substandard housing in 1960 was twice as large in the South as in the rest of the country.

The Link with Population Characteristics

Overcrowding is linked to race at each level of low income included in Appendix 16; throughout, the non-white inhabit dwellings with the higher person-per-room ratios. At each low-income level they also have more than the average likelihood of occupying dilapidated buildings, as Appendix 17 indicates. The Negro slum ghetto appears as a

---

1. This census classification for isolating a truly metropolitan economy includes the central city, the city's suburbs, and sometimes adjacent rural areas.

feature of American life not eradicable by simple income changes. It is a feature as visible in non-urban as in urban areas. Appendix 19 shows that in 1960 only 17 per cent of housing units occupied by non-whites and located outside SMSA's were in sound condition with all plumbing; 64 per cent were dilapidated or deteriorated. Inside SMSA's the majority of non-whites inhabited housing units that were physically sound and had plumbing, but the ratio of 56.8 per cent must be compared with that of 83.1 per cent for the general population within SMSA's.

The aged poor as a group tend to occupy bad, albeit not over-crowded housing. Appendix 20 shows the 1960 distribution of housing conveniences among recipients of Old Age Assistance. A large segment of this group in 1960 lacked even one flush toilet to a family; many lived without running water. Electricity, the most widespread of the modern conveniences, however, was enjoyed by almost all beneficiaries. Again, non-whites fared worse in all categories. [1]

Health and Housing

Bad housing is related to a large number of diseases of the poor, discussed in detail in the next section. Here we may note the relation of specific diseases to poor housing. Time and again the high correlation between tuberculosis and a high person-per-room ratio has been found.

Lead poisoning among the very young and the very old poor is the direct result of dilapidated housing whose chipped lead paint enters the body. [2]

Studies which compare the condition of the poor before and after their resettlement to better housing throw additional light on the relationship of housing to disease. In a recent investigation a controlled group of new occupants of public housing was studied in depth and contrasted with a test group who remained in the slums. The expectation that the rehoused group would have lower illness rates was borne out in part. In general, those under 35 years of age, especially children, showed the more favorable rate; but the disease pattern did not affect all groups equally. For instance, those under 20 had fewer infections

1. Characteristics and Financial Circumstances of Recipients of Old-Age Assistance 1960, Part I, National Data, p. 12.

2. "Death for Children Lurks in Walls of Old and Run-Down Housing," Journal of Housing, February 1958, pp. 59, 60, 72.

and parasitic conditions as well as fewer digestive troubles and far fewer accidents than those who were not rehoused. The project children had an accident rate about one-third lower than the slum children. But the the health of the children did not improve immediately upon rehousing— in fact, there was a higher rate of illness during the initial period, which was attributed to a lack of group immunity to common communicable diseases. On the other hand, adults between the ages of 20 and 34 had no fewer respiratory and digestive ills but, unexpectedly, had a lower incidence of a wide range of allergic, endocrine, metabolic, circulatory, and mental disorders. Housing seemed to have little effect upon the rates of illness of those over 35. [1]

Improved housing may bring about other improvements. Probably the more crucial ones are attitudinal and help shape the quality of aspirations. The correlation of better housing with school performance— at least in terms of proportions in the dropout age still in school—is indicated in Appendix 21, which shows that a greater proportion of school-age children living in housing projects stay in school than of those in adjoining neighborhoods, even though their families' incomes are slightly lower.

The New School's study thus did not discover any direct and unique causal link between poor housing and poverty. What is clear is that the poor live in very bad housing and that the nation's housing deficit is a large one. Yet if it has been found that housing is only part of the story of poverty, should its role be ignored? Obviously not, as good housing stands by itself as a worthwhile goal of social policy.

1. Daniel M. Wilner et al., The Housing Environment and Family Life: A Longitudinal Study of the Effects of Housing on Morbidity and Mental Health, Johns Hopkins Press, Baltimore, 1962.

10

Health and poverty

T H E   L E V E L of a nation's over-all health is related to its economic progress, its public health policy, its level of education, and housing. Over the years, improved public health services and preventive inoculation have particularly benefited the poor in the United States, as in other countries.

Differentials in health remain between upper and lower income levels. The poor are particularly prone to certain diseases, especially those associable with poor housing or the lack of immunization. They are more likely to suffer from accidents characteristic of hazardous occupations and from mental disability. Thus, the U. S. National Health Survey, 1957-58,[1] found the following variations in number of days of disability according to income class:

	Below $2,000	$2,000- $4,000	$4,000- $7,000
Restricted activity days per person	32.4	20.5	16.5
Bed disability days per person	12.2	7.8	6.9
Days in hospital per hospitalized person	11.7	8.5	7.2
Days of work-loss due to injury per usually working person	3.8	2.4	1.1

The somewhat poorer health of the poor may be due to the fact that superior health—in the aggregate—is purchasable. Having less to buy health with, the poor have less health. Better health among the higher income groups may also result from better knowledge of hygiene among the educated. Ill and disabled persons are more likely to be unable to earn a good living. Whatever the reason, there is a demonstrable statistical connection between low income and poor health. This connection appears to hold even when age is held constant in the comparisons and when diseases and disabilities not broadly known as linked to income are compared by income level. The variety of the data studied by the staff of the New School poverty study and the adjustments

1. U.S. National Health Survey, Health Statistics, Series B-7, B-8, B-10, 1960.

made to correct the data for demographic differences are not reported
on in detail. Even if the link between low income and disease were not
corrected for age, race, and the other poverty-linked characteristics,
the very existence of the association would still be an important datum
for policy. We have seen earlier that what is crucial in the understand-
ing of poverty in an affluent society is precisely that terms such as
"Negro," "aged," "uneducated," and "sick" can increasingly be sub-
stituted for the term "poor."

The data surveyed revealed that the link between health and income
depends very much on what level of low income is chosen. In terms of
the highest level of our band of poverty—"minimum comfort," or what
others have called "deprivation"—the association is tenuous.

Incidence of Specific Diseases

Pulmonary disease is clearly related to poor housing conditions,
especially among non-whites. Mortality from pneumonia and influenza,
as well as the distribution of active cases of pneumonia, show non-
whites to be affected more than twice as much as whites. In New York
City, for instance, the incidence of tuberculosis among Negroes in
1961, measured by the rate of new cases, stood at 158.2 per 100,000
against a rate of 32.9 among whites; the Puerto Rican rate was 98.9.[1]
These data relating to the pulmonary diseases—against which much
progress has been made—indicate how the association between poverty
and disease operates, as indicated earlier, by way of congested housing.

Lower rates of immunization among the poorer population appear
to explain the heavier impact on the poor of poliomyelitis, diphtheria,
whooping cough, and other diseases for which immunization is opera-
tive. Low-income families appear not to avail themselves of the opportunity to be vaccinated, and this fact does not seem to be due to cost.

It appears that cancer incidence in the lowest income group is above
the average and that among men aged 20 to 64 cancer of the esophagus,
mouth, and pharynx are inversely related to income, as are stomach
and lung cancer.[2]

1. See Control of the Communicable Diseases, Health Information Foundation,
April 1957; Anthony M. Lowell, Tuberculosis in New York City, 1961, New York
City Tuberculosis and Health Association, 1962, p. 15.

2. H. F. Dorn and S. J. Cutler, "Morbidity from Cancer in the U. S.," Public
Health Monograph No. 56, U. S. Public Health Service, 1959. P. Buell, J. E.
Dunn, Jr., and L. Breslow, "The Occupational-Social Class Risks of Cancer Mor-
tality in Men," Journal of Chronic Diseases, December 1960, pp. 600-21. Ed-
ward M. Cohart, "Socioeconomic Distribution of Stomach Cancer in New Haven,"
Cancer, July 1954, pp. 455-61; and "Socio-economic Distribution of Cancer of the
Lung in New Haven," Cancer, November-December 1955, pp. 1126-29.

The poor suffer more from arthritis, syphilis, diseases of the female genital organs, and heart disease. Members of higher income brackets appear to suffer more from diabetes mellitis. (See Appendix 22.)

The Disabled

Disability, as is well known, is responsible for the limited employability of many Americans. The disabled are apparently predominantly middle aged. More than three out of four of the recipients of federal-state Aid to the Permanently and Totally Disabled (APTD), according to a 1951 survey, were at least 45 years old; one out of every three was at least 60. For at least 57 per cent, more than five years had elapsed since the onset of their major impairment. Eight out of ten had impairments due to chronic diseases or congenital conditions. About one-fourth of the disabled suffered from heart disease. Three out of five were afflicted by more than one disease. The disability rate for Negroes was twice that of whites.[1]

The Poor Start with Poor Health

As predictable, available data indicate that low income is a barrier to the use of preventive medical service. At all ages and all educational levels persons and families earning less than $2,000 per year had significantly less frequent physician's visits.[2] The ratio of frequency of physician's visits showed a higher inverse correlation to education than to income. Utilization of immunization, pediatric,[3] and dental services[4] was also found to be related to income—the lower the income the less were such facilities used. Adjusting the data for education narrowed the income effect but did not do away with it.

1. Characteristics of Recipients of Aid to the Permanently and Totally Disabled, Mid-1951, Public Assistance Report No. 22, U.S. Department of Health, Education, and Welfare, April 1953.

2. U.S. Department of Health, Education, and Welfare, Public Health Bulletin No. 19, 1960.

3. Laughton, Buck and Holb, "Socioeconomic Status and Illness," Millbank Memorial Fund Quarterly, January 1958, pp. 46-54.

4. Public Health Bulletin No. 15.

Causality here does not operate only through lack of income. Significant are the failure of the poor to identify minor symptoms, their more limited knowledge of hygiene, and their lesser use even of free medical facilities.

Beyond the recognition that the poor have less preventive care lies the question of whether the poor in their pre-disease condition are disadvantaged by some kind of inherent weakness—what in the nineteenth century was called "poor protoplasm." To probe this question data on infant mortality, diseases of children, and the physical characteristics of the poor were surveyed.

The close correlation between high infant mortality and low income observable throughout the world has been ascribed to poor nutrition, ignorance, and overcrowding. In the United States, the historical trend, in terms of children dying in the first year of life per each 1,000 live births, has been downward from 162.4 in 1900, 75.4 in 1925, 29.2 in 1950, to 26.0 in 1960.

Higher infant mortality rates are noted in non-white areas of major U.S. cities. In 1960, in New York City, for instance, in heavily non-white and Puerto Rican slum areas, rates were exceptionally high; central Harlem reported 146.6 per cent of the over-all average for the city, and the Bedford section of Brooklyn reported 137.7 per cent. Manhattan, on the whole more heavily non-white than the other boroughs of New York, had a rate 28.5 per cent higher than the average for the five boroughs.[1] Anderson[2] suggests that the current level of infant mortality is, at least in part, due to the presence within the population of a core of mothers who are "non-copers," the loss of whose children can be explained as reflecting lack of ability and training in "mothercraft." The absence of mothercraft is not necessarily entirely a function of the educational level of the mothers nor of the economic status of the family. It may reflect the presence of psychological problems which a mere change in education would not overcome, or of a style of life that hinders the transmission of the art from mother to daughter.

Recent studies have noted how infant mortality rates in the United States, while low in comparison with those of all other nations, have not improved as rapidly as in many of the industrialized Western coun-

1. Summary of Vital Statistics, City of New York, Department of Health, 1960, Table 12, p. 10.

2. Odin W. Anderson, "Infant Mortality and Social Cultural Factors, Historical Trends and Current Patterns," in Patients, Physicians and Illness, E. Gartely Jaco, ed., Free Press, Glencoe, 1958.

tries. This slowdown in the rate of improvement in the infant mortality statistics, particularly marked in the decade of the fifties, is due to a multitude of causes. What is significant is that in 1959 and 1960 the pattern of New York City was repeated, with even greater increases, in eight of this country's ten largest cities. This is in line with the increase in the number of the poor in large urban centers and with the increasing proportion of non-whites in these low-income populations. In addition to less knowledge of "mothercraft," what contributes to the higher infant mortality of the poor are the lesser availability of prenatal care of the low-income populations (data show that in poor neighborhoods only 4 out of 10 mothers have prenatal care while in the non-poor neighborhoods 7 out of 10 mothers have prenatal care), the crowded facilities, and the fact that prenatal clinics to which the poor are admitted are inaccessible as they are rarely located in poor neighborhoods. Non-whiteness itself does not explain the higher rates. Indeed, various studies have shown that at higher income levels non-white women and white women have the same prematurity and infant mortality rates. [1]

To investigate the non-somatic aspects of the extent to which the poor start life disadvantaged, post-neonatal rates (i.e., deaths between the ages of one month and one year) appear useful. Indeed, the poverty link, if any, would show up in the care of children rather than in the biological accident of death within the first month of life. In 1958 post-neonatal rates for the total population ranged very widely among states and between whites and non-whites. The existing spread was investigated in terms of the link to income as well as the link to education. The resulting correlation was particularly strong for the non-white population where the correlation with income was negative and significant and the correlation with low education was positive and significant. [2]

The child of the poor, whether physically less well endowed at birth or because of early environmental effects, is sick more often than his contemporary higher on the economic scale. Particularly

1. Ibid.

2. The correlation was calculated for thirty states (including the District of Columbia). Those states in which the non-whites made up less than 2.5 per cent of the population and those in which the Indian population was more than 60 per cent of the non-whites were left out. These latter five (Arizona, Montana, New Mexico, North and South Dakota) were omitted because the mortality rates were far out of line with the others. These extremes are explained in part by differences in general standards of health care among the various non-white groups. The value of the correlation with income was -.701, that with low education was +.724.

significant are the findings of a study[1] in which the illness rate of in-
fants under age 2 of low-income parents was more than twice the rate
of those in the upper income group. This is in spite of the fact that
the entire population under study was covered by comprehensive prepaid medical care.

The link between poverty and bad health is traditionally pursued
also by comparison of the physical characteristics of children, such
as weight, height, and chest measurements. When Rowntree in his
three studies on poverty in York, for instance, compared the height
and weight of children 5 to 13 years of age in three social classes
(poorest, middle, highest), the correlation between poverty and low
height and weight was impressive. Similar studies in the United States
go back as far as 1875. Although their results are not as striking as
the Rowntree findings, they permit us to draw roughly the same conclusions on the correlation between bodily characteristics and socio-
economic status.

All the studies reviewed by the New School research staff agree
that at the middle-childhood ages both boys and girls of the lower income classes are significantly shorter and lighter in weight than those
of the higher income classes. They also show that over the years increases in height have been greater and increases in weight have been
less among the children of the poor than among the children of the economically more favored.[2]

The Cost of Medical Care

The increase in the quality, availability, and use of U. S. medical
services since 1920 has brought with it an unprecedented rise in costs.
These increased costs must be viewed against the changes that have
also taken place in the earnings of the low-income population.

The significance of the medical price spiral is clarified when we
see that the increase between 1953 and 1958 in the mean gross charges
per family for personal health services was only 16 per cent in the
family income class $7,500 and over, compared with 30 per cent in
the $5,000-$7,499 income class, 39 per cent in the $3,500-$4,999 class
and 49 per cent in the $2,000-$3,499 class. Among families with in-

1. Laughton, Buck and Holb, op. cit.

2. Hundley et. al., "Height and Weight of First-Grade Children as a Potential
Index of Nutritional Status," American Journal of Public Health, 1955, pp. 1454-
61.

come less than $2,000 the increase was 27 per cent.[1] Thus the poor
are hit hardest by increased medical costs. And their situation is
worse yet because on the average they need more care. The situation
holds for all the low-income groups within the band of poverty. Forty-
four per cent of families earning less than $5,000 at the end of the
1950's were reported as having serious problems because of medical
expenses.[2] The aged, living on fixed and low income and needing more
care, felt the rise in costs more than any other group. Poverty in the
affluent society often hides its face behind a mask of retirement plans,
public and private. From afar those over 65 appear to be secure in a
structure of Social Security checks, Railroad Retirement payments,
private pension benefits, and hospitalization schemes. A closer view
shows the structure's true foundation. Again costs and needs are
greatest where incomes are lowest. The seriousness of the discrepancy is exemplified best in the fact that average private medical expenditures in 1960 for those over 65 amounted to $207. In that year
half of all persons 65 and over had less than $870 in total income.[3]

Distribution of Health Insurance

The phenomenal growth of voluntary health and hospital insurance
schemes in the postwar years gave multitudes of factory and office
workers protection against the economic threat of medical bills. But
the new institutional arrangements do not suffice for either the poor
or the old. The extent of coverage, by income class, of the various
forms of insurance, as of the end of 1959, is summarized in Appendix 23. Only one-third of families with income below $2,000 were cov-
ered by hospital insurance and a little more than one-fourth by surgi-
cal insurance, compared with half or more of families in higher income
categories having such protection. Medical insurance was held by 9
per cent of the poorest families, 14 per cent of families with income
of $2,000-$4,000, 22 per cent of those with income of $4,000-$7,000.
When the data are corrected for age, the percentages decrease some-

1. U.S. Bureau of the Census, Statistical Abstract of the United States, 1964,
derived from Table 88, p. 73.

2. Family Spending Patterns and Health Care, Health Information Foundation,
January 1960, p. 5.

3. Herman M. and Anne R. Somers, Doctors, Patients and Health Insurance,
The Brookings Institution, Washington, 1962, pp. 429-31.

what in all income categories; the most marked decrease takes place
among families in the less than $2,000 income class. But again, the
age-corrected data do not change the story. Those with group health
plans face sharply reduced coverage as well as substantial rises in
new-insurance cost when they retire.[1] Individual policies are more
expensive, persons who are considered poor risks may be excluded,
contracts can be cancelled. Thus, for one reason or another, only one
out of two of the non-institutionalized aged with less than $4,000 a year
family income was covered by any hospital insurance at all in 1959.[2]

The aged are particularly vulnerable to continuing medical costs.
Chronic illnesses require medical attention and expensive drugs, but
rarely surgery or hospitalization. With the passage of Medicare, the
situation of the elderly poor will improve.

Mental Disability

That there is a statistically observable link between poverty and
mental disease is known—a strikingly high number of persons admitted
to state and private hospitals for mental disorders come from slum
areas.[3] And among one disadvantaged group, non-whites, the average
hospitalization rate for mental illness is double that of the population
as a whole.[4]

The statistics are clear, but the relationship between poor mental
health and bad environment is not. Does mental disability lead downward to the slums? Or does slum life accentuate tendencies toward
mental ill health?

The belief that mental illness has prevented large numbers of psy-

1. The Health Care of the Aged: Background Facts Relating to the Financing
Problems, Social Security Administration, Division of Program Research, 1962.

2. Ibid., Table 26, p. 163. Data are for July to December 1959; the situation
may have changed somewhat in view of the drive in 1962 to extend coverage.

3. Robert Faris and H. Warren Dunham, Mental Disorders in Urban Areas,
University of Chicago Press, 1939; Clarence Schroder, "Mental Disorders in
Cities," American Journal of Sociology, July 1942, pp. 40-47; August B. Hollingshead and Fredrick C. Redlich, Social Class and Mental Illness: A Community Study, Wiley, New York, 1958; Leo Srole et al., Mental Health in the Metropolis: The Midtown Manhattan Study, McGraw-Hill, New York, 1962.

4. Benjamin Malzberg, "Mental Disease Among Negroes," Mental Hygiene,
July 1959, pp. 422 ff.

chotics from earning a living is known as the "drift hypothesis." Ac=
cording to this theory, economic failures from all walks of life drift
into the slums. Among these are many patients committed to mental
hospitals who give slum addresses. Their residence in the slums,
however, so the theory goes, may be the consequence, not the cause
of their illness.[1]

Another theory is that high rates of psychosis in the slums can be
ascribed, not to drift downward, but to residential immobility of the
mentally ill in areas from which the normal tendency is to move away.
Those who remain may represent a residue of particularly ill-adapted
persons. Hollingshead and Redlich, in their study cited above, found
a high degree of social immobility among schizophrenics also—the
overwhelming majority of treated schizophrenics in New Haven (91 per
cent) were in the same socio-economic class as their parents. In
Mental Health in the Metropolis, also cited above, Srole and his associates hypothesized that "on the whole, upward status mobility is
rewarding psychically as well as materially, whereas downward status
mobility is depriving in both respects."

The New School poverty study staff surveyed the link between poverty and mental health at length. It hopes to report the findings at a
later date and in a different context. Suffice it to say that the study
staff was impressed by the extent to which the link goes to specific
forms of mental disease—various forms of schizophrenia—rather than
to the general category of mental diseases. The staff was also impressed by its preliminary calculation as to the number of poor afflicted by mental disease of this type. The calculations are complex
and the data not very good. We can here report our judgment that, on
the basis of evidence available, the number of poor in the United States
who are thus afflicted can be estimated to be in excess of 2 million.

1. D.L. Gerard and L.G. Houston, "Family Setting and the Social Ecology
of Schizophrenia," Psychiatric Quarterly, 1953, pp. 90-101; E.H. Hare, "Mental
Illness and Social Condition in Bristol," Journal of Mental Science, 1956, pp. 349-
57; Rene Lapousse, Mark A. Monk, and Milton Terres, "The Drift Hypothesis and
Socioeconomic Differentials in Schizophrenia," American Journal of Public Health,
August 1956, p. 978.

11

The "displaced"
and the "never placed"

THE DEPRESSION of the 1930's was a major turning point in American economic history. At it, the moving finger stuck, leaving a large smudge called unemployment. Unlike the Civil War, that other major turning point, it left no part of the country and no individual untouched. With one person out of every five in the labor force out of work, unemployment became the great leveler and the great dread. More than any other period of this country's economic history, the Depression riveted unemployment into a synonym for poverty. With it, whether it involved the factory worker, the farmer or the businessman, the ethos that marked the unemployed as an inferior being regained a temporary hold: vulgarized forms of Social Darwinism received their final fillip.

The demoralization caused by unemployment cannot be minimized; young and old were willing to do "anything" but there was nothing for them to do. The impact on individuals, on the social structure, on the values of the society is well known and documented.[1] Its impact on contemporary and later economic policy is also well known. In the public's concentration on the problem of unemployment, poverty as such was almost lost sight of: in spite of the 33 million poor and the fact that average family income was below the contemporary poverty line, all energies were directed toward doing away with unemployment. With World War II, large-scale unemployment disappeared and, but for the legislation of 1946, which was the crucial, albeit belated, reaction to the previous decade, it vanished as a major policy concern. With it disappeared whatever latent policy concern with the problems of poverty might have existed. Unemployment became relegated to the substrata of the citizen's and the policy-maker's mind, now primarily concerned with inflation, growth, and the Cold War.

1. See, for example, Edward W. Bakke, Citizens Without Work (1939), and The Unemployed Worker (1940), both issued by Yale University Press, New Haven; Frederick L. Allen, The Big Change, Harper and Brothers, New York, 1952.

In recent years, unemployment has slowly regained public attention as aggregate unemployment rates have increased. Since 1957, approximately 5 per cent of the total labor force and usually about four
million individuals, more or less, have been the victims of frictional
(between-jobs), seasonal, cyclical, or structural unemployment.[1] Of
these, the growing total of long=term structurally unemployed—those
whose joblessness results from lasting changes in the U. S. economic,
demographic, and occupational structure—gives serious ground for
concern. These "displaced" and "never placed" people are prime can-
didates for permanent poverty. As the postwar period has progressed,
the unemployed have remained out of work for longer average periods
of time. While in 1947-49 the average duration of unemployment was
10 weeks or less (Appendix 26), by the end of the 1950's that figure
had climbed to 13 weeks (with a peak of 15. 5 weeks in 1961).[2] At the
beginning of 1965, aggregate unemployment approached 4 per cent.

Mass and Class Unemployment

Among specialists debate as to the level, nature, and causes of recent unemployment is rampant. There is disagreement as to whether
the unemployment of the affluent society is cyclical or structural,
whether it is due to changes in the structure of demand for products
or in the structure of the labor force, to an "excessively high social
wage" or to the competition from imports from certain low-wage nations. Future prospects are also unclear. But there is much that is
very clear.

Increasingly, unemployment, like poverty, is less a matter of individuals and more a matter of special groups. It strikes at much the
same groups as poverty: Negroes, the young, the aged. In the 1950's,
unemployment also began to strike more frequently at non-whites, the
young, the unskilled, and the poorly educated (Appendix 27), and, in
an historically symptomatic change, manufacturing workers.

Consider youth, for example, as a poverty-linked and sometimes
an unemployment-linked characteristic. At the beginning of the 1950's,
for each male unemployed worker in the prime working age (25 to 44),
there were about 2. 9 unemployed males in the 14 to 19 age group. At

1. The seasonally adjusted figure for July 1964 was 4. 9 per cent unemployed.
Employment and Earnings, U.S. Bureau of Labor Statistics, August 1964, Table
A-1, p. 1.

2. The figure for 1963-64 was between 11 and 13 weeks. Ibid., Table A-8,
p. 5.

the end of the decade, there were in the same age group more than 3.4 unemployed for each unemployed male in the prime age group.

The groups which suffered most in the 1950's from increased unemployment are also overrepresented among the long-term unemployed. In 1960 almost 17 per cent of unemployed non-white males were out of work longer than 27 weeks versus a national average of 11.5 per cent. Non-white males averaged 16.4 weeks between jobs versus the average figure for all male unemployed of 12.8 weeks.

Among occupational groups in the early 1960's operatives, service workers (other than domestic), and laborers (other than farm and mine) suffered the longest unemployment and made up a disproportionate part of the long-term unemployed. [1]

Long-term unemployment and differentiated unemployment rates are particularly characteristic of the depressed areas. Beckley, Bluefield, Hazard, Hagerstown, Huntington, Morgantown are scale models of depressed areas in the hundreds. Locations particularly hit by changes in demand or by changes in technology, they have unemployment rates at least twice the national level. In Hagerstown, Maryland, for example, the unemployment rate—one out of every six workers in 1960—almost matches the levels of the Great Depression. Here unemployment seems permanent; men and women have plenty of time on their hands, and, as long as they have the energy, use it to line up at the "unemployment office," at the surplus food distribution point or any place that offers the possibility of hope or aid.

Since 1961 about 800 areas have been classified as entitled to special assistance from the Economic Development Administration (formerly the ARA). Statistics for these areas are now available and can be integrated with data published earlier by the Department of Labor to provide some clues as to the impact of unemployment in the depressed areas upon the economy. Contrary to popular belief, they do not contribute significantly to the national totals. Indeed, the depressed areas are, with few exceptions, small. In the national total probably no more than one in twelve workers can be said to owe his idleness to this problem.

1. "Unemployment Rates and Percent Distribution of the Unemployed by Occupation Group, 1959-62," Table 1-4, U.S. Bureau of Labor Statistics, 1962 Statistical Supplement, Monthly Labor Review. Also the following Special Labor Force Reports in the Monthly Labor Review: "Work History, Attitudes, and Income of the Unemployed," by Robert L. Stein, issue of December 1963, pp. 1405-13; and "Geographical Mobility and Employment Status, March 1962-March 1963," by Samuel Saben, issue of August 1964, pp. 873-81. For figures on farm employment see reports of Statistical Reporting Service, U.S. Department of Agriculture.

In the depressed areas unemployment is more nearly akin to poverty than anywhere else in the United States. This is so because the
unemployed in these areas are predominantly in the poverty-linked
groups and because the poverty-linked groups make up so large a proportion of the population of the depressed areas. [1]

The mass unemployment of the 1930's has largely given way to
"class" unemployment in the 1950's and 1960's. Unlike mass unemployment, which primarily reflects cyclical economic variations, class
unemployment reflects more lasting social and technological forces.
Increased class unemployment measures the extent to which our society is rejecting and excluding an increasing number of its members.
It is here, in these individuals, that poverty and unemployment are
wedded.

The obviously direct relationship between fluctuations in unemployment and "non-earner" poverty was illustrated in the New School
study by correlating Pi coefficients for poverty, discussed earlier,
with unemployment rates. A positive correlation between these two
factors was found to exist at the highest of the three income levels used.
On the other hand, at the lower levels negative correlations were observed. [2] These correlations suggest that the effect of increased economic activity is felt by those in the upper part of the low income scale
but not by those living in abject poverty. Obviously, to be affected by
economic changes one has to be part of the economy. To become unemployed one has to have a job from which to become unemployed.
The number living in abject poverty is not strongly affected by economic fluctuations.

The relationship between the Pi coefficients of various individual
traits at different levels of poverty and aggregate levels of unemployment varies. In comparing unemployment among men aged 14 to 24
and the values of the Pi coefficient for families headed by men in this
age category, rough positive correlations are found at the two higher
levels of low income and none at the lowest level. A similar pattern
emerges for female family heads. Only when one looks at the picture
for family heads aged 65 and over does the correlation change. A negative relationship at the subsistence level is apparent, and no relationship at either of the two higher levels.

1. See Statistical Profile of Redevelopment Areas, U.S. Bureau of the Census,
Series SP, 1962.

2. If, at the "very low" and "middle low" levels the extraordinary years 1951
(high prosperity) and 1958 (deep recession) are excluded, the negative relationship
is even sharper. The height of the coefficients in 1951 is a reflection of the corresponding good conditions of the non-poor population, and the opposite is true in
1958, where the remainder of the population is worse off, thus making the Pi coefficient of the poor — since it is a relative factor — look low in comparison.

The picture becomes clearer when we consider recent labor force participation rates. Appendix 25 shows how in the 1950's the labor force participation of poverty-linked groups declined. As employment opportunities decreased, the very young, the very old, the non-whites, and those with only eight years or less of schooling became increasingly inactive in the economy. In the depressed areas, where aggregate economic participation—as expressed in labor force participation rates—is less than the national average, the very young men and the very old men had especially low rates of participation in 1960 (Appendix 24).

The poverty-linked groups, to the extent that they are old, non-whites, or unschooled, are displaced from our economy. Having no skill, they find no job; finding no job, they withdraw from the labor force.

How to Become Displaced in the Affluent Society

How does the displacement work? The displaced miner, earning $27 a day before he became unemployed, typifies many. Others are Negro meat packers formerly earning $2.25 an hour and fringe benefites; or displaced automobile workers too old to obtain work and too young to retire. Automation has not so far been the main cause of displacement, though evidence points to a very major future impact of automation. A general upgrading in employment requirements is as much, if not more, the cause of displacement.

Making a living today depends increasingly upon the possession of certain techniques, such as the ability to fill in questionnaires, to pass aptitude tests, to use the right words; and, more important even than techniques, formal education. Entry to jobs is increasingly determined by formal educational requirements which may or may not be related to the duties of the position.

The civil service in New York City, for instance, has made formal education a requirement for jobs which ten years previously did not make this demand—jobs as firemen, maintenance men, and elevator mechanic helpers, for example. The job content, both in its formal description and in reality, has not changed. For "Housing Officer," whose duty is to patrol the public spaces in buildings of the city public housing projects, formal education is now required. Throughout the New York City area, "compared with the declining printing and food processing industries, the rising radio and electronics field, fabricated metal manufacturing and electrical industries make greater use of educational attainment as a condition of hiring."[1]

1. Jerome Joffe, "Unemployment and Education," Master's thesis, The Graduate Faculty, New School for Social Research, 1963, pp. 16, 17.

Such developments repeated through the United States indicate the systematization of personnel management. They reflect a rise in managerial expectation, which is moving faster than the actual improvement in skills of the labor force.

Systematized hiring policies displace the old as effectively as lack of education and technological change displace the worker in the prime age group. Others are displaced by disease—mental and physical. Lastly, there is discrimination; it displaces workers more subtly than other factors, but probably more irrevocably.

The "Never Placed"

What of those not liable to displacement—the "never placed"?

A very significant drop in labor market participation is that of young males, a group particularly singled out by the unemployment of the 1950's and 1960's. The problem of unemployment among the young, particularly young men, is multi-faceted. It involves, for example, inadequate training and insufficient skills in an economy which calls for greater and greater skill and where employers of the young, as well as of the old, insist on high experience qualifications.

The Residuum

Marshall pointed to the presence of a "residuum" made up of "persons who are physically, mentally or morally incapable of doing a good day's work with which to earn a good day's wage" and called for prompt action.[1] The "residuum" is still with us, as is the call for action. Marshall's notion of the "residuum" was, however, a single one which assumed a "full" employment situation. In contemporary America there are actually two residua, that of the economy and that of the society, which overlap and interact: both involve a notion of "incapacity," the incapacity being external to the individual as well as internal. Both residua partake of a traditional incapacity—the weakness of the individual's endowment or training—and a new incapacity—the structural rejection.

The "structural" poor are also a "residuum" but they are society's, more than the economy's, "residuum." The demographic and income changes reported upon earlier—the non-income aspects of poverty—can also be described as resulting from structural changes.

1. Alfred Marshall, Principles of Economics, 9th edition, Macmillan, New York, 1961, p. 714.

Changes in the make-up of the poor broadly reflect forces affecting structural changes in unemployment. The two obviously interact and overlap, yet, as in the case of Negro poverty, they are different.

In a society where the economic system is working relatively efficiently, poverty and unemployment are linked in a very different fashion from where it is not. The richer society calls for a framework of analysis significantly different from the traditional one and for a discussion of policy that recognizes this fact.

The data needed for a detailed discussion of policies, Marshall's "prompt action in regard to the large, though it may be hoped now steadily diminishing residuum," were studied and are reported upon in the third and final part of this summary. Here, some preliminary observations are in order. Policy cannot be based on the assumption that poverty is an "afterthought," as Galbraith would suggest, or on the equally extreme position of his critic Kolko, who argues that "the basic economic fact of life for a majority of the population is insecurity."[1] Policy must be formulated in recognition of both affluence and poverty. Public policies on unemployment must similarly recognize both the problems of level and the problems of structure.

The primacy of class unemployment calls for action along a variety of particularized and specific lines. Some of these are catalogued later in this report. They are related to education, training, and retraining activities within the local, state, federal, and private systems.

The experience with class unemployment of the past decade belies the notion that "The most effective remedy for all economic maladjustments causing structural or chronic unemployment is a healthy rate of economic growth. Under such conditions some readjustments take place more or less automatically; others can be achieved more easily ...."[2] The contrary is the case. As we have seen, economic growth, reflected in increased aggregate employment, has not led to more or less automatic readjustment in the level of unemployment of the groups suffering from chronic unemployment. As tools, monetary and fiscal policies are inadequate for dealing with every type of unemployment and stratified structural poverty. Specific policy tools, proper statistics, and special programs are required. Apart from the inadequacy of tools geared to full employment there is no reason to believe that our society can easily achieve those levels of employment—if any such exist—that could theoretically do away with class unemployment and poverty.

1. Gabriel Kolko, Wealth and Power in America, Praeger, New York, 1962, p. 129.

2. The Rise of Chronic Unemployment, Board of Trustees, National Planning Association, April 1961, Pamphlet No. 113, p. 3.

The need for multiple policies in no way detracts from the importance of a national economic policy geared to the lowering of aggregate unemployment and the achievement of high levels of economic growth, individual income, and so on. To realize society's full employment goals, monetary and fiscal policies are appropriate and adequate. On the other hand, even their timely and energetic use is not sufficient to deal with the problem of class unemployment and its poverty correlates.

In all policy decisions a number of objectives must be considered and ranked. The current situation, as far as the relationship between poverty and unemployment is concerned, establishes one inescapable parameter: whatever the ultimate ranking, traditional means of pursuing a "full employment policy" are not enough.

12

Poverty and the labor market, old and new

CONTEMPORARY poverty cannot be explained altogether in terms of groups with high poverty risks, or in terms of the convergence of poverty-linked characteristics. Structural unemployment and underemployment account for part of the poverty-stricken population. There also exist situations in which neither the lack of jobs nor the characteristics of individuals are a sufficient explanation. The poverty of the small inefficient farmer, the poverty of the worker in the sweatshop and those paid the statutory minima or less, that of the migrant farm worker and of a few independent businessmen relate to the peculiarity of the labor market.

The market as the clearing house and balancer of needs and satisfactions and as the allocator of private and social goods and services has always operated imperfectly. In the affluent society, increased possibilities of choice, the greater variety in conception of needs, have, in peculiar fashion, made the market both more and less effective than where the "bondage of extreme scarcity, ... the fierceness of competition" force the masses to a close economic calculus.[1] Having freed the bulk of the masses from the bondage of extreme scarcity, the current economic and social mechanism permits the occasional giving way to capriciousness and condones the systematizing of irrationalities. As hunger does not stalk the land, the social interstices, in which the individual finds a "niche" where his earnings are not a fair measure of his contributions, have enlarged.

Economic sectors with many low-income families and individuals have often been found by the New School staff to be sectors with marginal employers, small capital investments, and inadequate social regulation. Here the market works, but with a considerable lag.

---

1. Cf. Robert L. Heilbroner, The Making of Economic Society, Prentice-Hall, Englewood Cliffs, 1962, p. 229 et passim; Adolph Lowe, "Comment on the Practical Uses of Theory," Social Research, Summer 1954, pp. 163-64.

Agriculture

The poverty-linked characteristic "rural farm residence" has already been noted. But from it, it does not follow that agriculture as such is linked to poverty.

For one thing, many are classified as farmers in the Census of Agriculture simply because they have a few acres from which they earn a little income. Thus, there were in a recent year at least 350,000 families on very small farms whose income from farm operation was primarily in kind and whose cash receipts, on the average, came mainly from off-farm work. As a group, these so-called farmers averaged about $450 during the year from the sale of farm products and a little over $500 in off-farm earnings.[1]

To a degree, farm poverty is the poverty of the aged, the unskilled and poorly educated, the non-whites and the southern residents. The Census of Agriculture provides information on the demographic characteristics of families on farms classed according to the value of products sold per year. Families with more of the poverty-linked characteristics appear close to the bottom of the lowest classes, ranging down to $50. Where incomes are somewhat higher, we note a greater proportion of individuals of prime working age, a higher educational achievement of children and parents, and a greater ability to earn from outside agriculture.[2]

The aging of the population engaged in agriculture is illuminating. The median age of farm operators, tenants, and sharecroppers has been rising gradually since the beginning of the century. In 1960, the population throughout farming aged 65 and over made up a larger group than the age bracket 25-34.[3] The aging of the farm population is particularly marked among farmers whose income places them well within the poverty band. For this group, almost 65 per cent of the farms are operated by persons 45 years of age and over.

---

1. Food and Agriculture: A Program for the 1960's, U.S. Department of Agriculture, 1962, p. 50.

2. See, for example, "Incomes of Rural Families in North East Texas," Texas Agricultural Experiment Stations, Bulletin No. 940. October 1959.

3. Herman W. Ruttan, "The Human Resource Problem in American Agriculture," in Farming, Farmers and the Market for Farm Goods, Committee for Economic Development, Supplementary Paper No. 15, November 1962, p. 79. Within the 65-and-over group, the proportion of individuals reported as farm operators has declined since 1954, when the availability of Social Security coverage permitted their formal retirement.

Poor farmers are not concentrated only among operators of small farms; they are remarkably concentrated geographically: well over half of the nation's low-income farm families are located in the South. [1]

A special factor dragging down the average income levels in agriculture is the low wage scale of hired farm workers, particularly migrants. Their earnings are reviewed later in this section along with those in other low-wage industries.

Part of farm poverty is the poverty of natural resources, the lack of irrigation, and soil erosion. But, again, this is not enough of an explanation for the bulk of farm poverty. Thus, the Georgia "broiler industry" developed in a typical area of rural poverty, yet in this instance poverty was done away with. [2]

At the heart of the problem of agricultural poverty is the increasing differential, insufficiently recognized, between the return from capital investment and that from hand labor. Says Higbee: "The vast outlay of capital required to enable a man to earn $2,500 from his own labor as a farmer is one of the basic facts of modern agriculture ... Because labor income is so low in agriculture, the difference between farmers who are poor and those who are well off is due chiefly to their capital resources and therefore to the amounts of income which they derive from capital invested." [3] It matters little whether the person involved is an owner-operator or a hired worker; unless the farm has a substantial investment in the latest machinery and equipment, in fertilizers and pesticides, in improved varieties of seeds and superior livestock, his income will be low and he will have little chance of continuous employment.

The paradox of abundance alongside extreme poverty in American agriculture leads Higbee to note: "It is ironic that within that very segment of the economy which suffers from the overproduction of food, there are farmers and farmhands who suffer from malnutrition because they cannot afford to eat properly." [4] The irony needs stressing, as too often all of agriculture is seen as poor while in fact it is not. A lot of talk about the "poor farmer," Higbee reminds us, stems from

---

1. Ibid., pp. 80-82.

2. Kenneth L. Bachman, "Economics of the Low Income Farm Problem," Journal of Farm Economics, December 1955, pp. 1408-16.

3. Edward Higbee, Farms and Farmers in an Urban Age, The Twentieth Century Fund, New York, 1963, p. 48.

4. Ibid., p. 11.

treating part-time, undercapitalized operators on small marginal plots
of land as though they were the principal factors in today's production
of food and fiber. The statistics of the agricultural sector, a sector
of American life which more than any other reflects the impact of new
knowledge and new technology and which may be at the very heart of
America's affluence, reminded the New School poverty study staff of
Alice and the Queen. Surely if a farmer is poor today and he has none
of the other poverty-linked characteristics that have been analyzed he
is not running fast enough!

Distressed Areas

It has been noted that "As his first executive action on becoming
President of the richest nation on earth, John F. Kennedy doubled the
quantity of flour, corn meal, dried milk, and other surplus commodi-
ties that the federal government is today distributing to some three
million needy Americans, and subsequently added pork and dried beans
to the ration."[1] The three million Americans who benefited from this
action live in the nation's depressed areas—areas which now qualify
for federal aid under a variety of schemes meant to encourage regional
development.

While important, unemployment cannot be said to be the central
problem of these distressed areas. Underemployment of labor better
characterizes their poverty. These are areas of depleted resources,
inadequate public and private investment, where large groups of individuals could be removed with no significant loss of output.

The principal reason for the poverty of a large number of depressed areas is insufficient out-migration. The distressed areas
are indeed losing population, and males both young and old are leaving them more rapidly than females.[2] The average age of the people
remaining is rising, with the 45-64 age group growing at a rate almost
25 per cent above the national average. These are apparently populations which suffer from below-average social services, particularly
in education.[3] In some cases the rebuilding and development of local

1. John Davenport, "In the Midst of Plenty," Fortune, March 1961, p. 107.

2. Vincent F. Gegan and Samuel H. Thompson, "Worker Mobility in a Labor
Surplus Area," Monthly Labor Review, December 1957, pp. 1451-56.

3. Characteristics of the Low Income Population, Joint Economic Committee
Staff Report, 84th Cong., 1st sess., 1955, pp. 156-85.

industries creates new opportunities. For most areas, it does not. Here organized out-migration is often opposed, on the pretext that the workers would reject it, by politicians who do not want to accept a shrinking electorate. Out-migration as a solution to the problem of distressed areas is also discouraged by a tendency to exaggerate the amount of it required to balance employment opportunities with labor supply. Our computation leads us to conclude that no more than 10 per cent of the labor force from each area need be involved in such out-migration.

Yet out-migration cannot be the only solution for the distressed areas. Underemployment of labor, and the poverty that it stands for, is here actually the result of other deficiencies. Entrepreneurial drive, effective capital availability, technical know-how, all lag badly behind the national norm in the depressed areas of Appalachia. Here a shortage of roads, power, and other forms of public investment denote the lack of social infrastructure typical of the underdeveloped nations of the world. Here poverty is the poverty of underdevelopment— the productivity of the region is just not enough to go around—it is not the poverty of the affluent society.

Low-Wage Industries

In economies of mid-development—those which have not reached a stage of high consumption—labor is always paid extremely low wages. It is out of the experience with such markets that earlier economists asserted their belief that the poverty of the working class stemmed from the fact of low wages. But the equation "wage earner equals being poor" is inappropriate in the affluent society. Current average weekly earnings of $102.97[1] for manufacturing production workers make it impossible to consider the wage earner per se as "poor." The annual income, assuming a sole earner in a family of four, would place the families of these workers within the "poverty band" as defined and reported upon earlier. However, the income would be equivalent to the "minimum comfort" standard. Here inclusion of such earners in the poverty group, while valid in some cases, seems to force the definition into the fallacy of misplaced concreteness. Workers in the "low-wage industries," on the other hand, do account for many of the poor.

What are the low-wage industries? Appendix 2, Table B, presents an index prepared by the New School poverty study staff of aver-

1. Data for July 1964; Employment and Earnings, August 1964, U.S. Bureau of Labor Statistics, p. 42.

age wages since the early 1900's in U.S. low-wage industries such as textiles, lumber and wood, and unskilled common labor on railroads and elsewhere. This "men's low-wage index," to which we had occasion to refer earlier, appears to have fallen rather consistently just above the contemporary "subsistence" level of the poverty band.

Estimated average hourly wages in seventeen low-paying industries in 1960 are shown in Appendix 29. Behind the averages are wide geographic differentials. The estimated number of workers earning less than $150 an hour in 1960 was over 8 million (Appendix 30).

Nothing is known with precision about the age or family make-up of workers in low-wage industries as a group. Certain trades, such as retail trade and the garment industry, tend to attract mostly women, many single. The hotel and restaurant trades are said to attract unattached elderly males. For the others, nothing is known as to their demographic characteristics. Assuming that in these industries, unattached individuals represent twice their proportion in the total labor force, [1] and therefore account for 3.2 million (40 per cent), and that of the workers living with their families, 46 per cent need not support anybody and account for another 2.2 million, there are still in this group at least 2.6 million workers who—even if employed on a full-time full-year basis—do not earn enough to bring them and their families to "minimum subsistence" levels. For these roughly 3 million and their families, this means abject poverty.

One extremely low-wage group is the large number of hired farm laborers, including many migrant workers, for whom there is a dwindling labor market need. A sample study of migrant workers in south Texas in 1958 showed that even with five persons working, average earnings per household were barely over $3,000 a year. [2]

Apart from Alaska, Hawaii, and Puerto Rico, none of which employs migrant workers, all states specifically exclude farm workers from minimum-wage laws, as does the federal government.

Surveying average earnings of migrant farm workers—cash earnings only, without allowance for the value of perquisites received—brings out that in 1959, for example, they averaged about $910 for the whole year, as against about $1,060 for non-migrant hired farm workers. The average annual earnings of migrant farm workers as a group

1. See Jacob Schiffman, Marital and Family Characteristics of Workers, March, 1960, Special Labor Force Report No. 13, U.S. Department of Labor, 1961, p. 3.

2. Background Data on the Migrant Worker Situation in the United States Today, Subcommittee on Migratory Labor, U.S. Senate Committee on Labor and Public Welfare, 86th Cong., 2nd sess., 1960, pp. 53-54.

are depressed by the low wages and intermittent employment of women (and to a lesser degree by children's low earnings too); yearly earnings of female workers in 1959 were less than half those of male workers. Occasional non-farm earnings do not add significantly to migrants' income as farm workers. In 1959 they contributed about $200 to their total for the year.[1]

The poverty of migratory workers, as that of the other categories discussed in this section, reflects inherent seasonality, lagging technology, and insufficient social regulation.

Low-wage workers employed in agriculture and other industries, and in some depressed areas in which these industries are located, are mostly unskilled; their attachment to the market is casual. They earn less than workers of comparable demographic, social, and skill characteristics in other endeavors.

For such sectors of the economy the market can be said to work effectively insofar as it selects workers of lesser capabilities and assigns many of them to inefficient producers. It can be said not to work insofar as competition does not immediately drive these employers out of business. At the heart of underemployment lies both a lagging adjustment to changes in technology and demand and a sluggishness in worker mobility.

1. The Hired Farm Working Force of 1959, U.S. Department of Agriculture, Agriculture Information Bulletin No. 238, p. 42.

PART THREE

13

The commitment to remedy

WHETHER poverty is viewed as social condition or as economic idea, insufficiency or inequality, objective economic conditions influence thought and action. Two corollaries emerge. As conditions have changed, poverty is seen as a "relative manner." And since poverty is "relative," standards of want reflect subjective estimates about which differences of opinion will always exist.

Analysis of the work of Booth and Rowntree and the study of workers' budgets reported on in Part One underline these variations. As variations occur from time to time in any one place, so do economic achievements vary from place to place. Of this we are continually apprised as we hear discussion of the problems of underdeveloped economies. Life for the poor in the United States today, it could easily be demonstrated, is far superior to that of the average Indian, Egyptian, or Chinese peasant. Few Americans are starving—though the life expectancy of some is lower than that of others because of malnutrition, unsanitary housing, inadequate health and education, and other factors.

Yet to establish that poverty is relative is a limited achievement. To know that there is no poverty in York of the type described by Rowntree in 1899 does not stop the unemployed of York from demonstrating outside Parliament. To be aware that life for some U.S. Negroes has improved does not keep the mob from rioting in Harlem or Rochester. The realization that a wealthy country does not require the same massive economic reconstruction as a poor one does not advance wisdom or policy. What is required is to trace social progress made toward removal of poverty.

Commitment to remedy in the United States is vouchsafed in a multitude of governmental and private actions, in the hundred thousand private welfare organizations, and in public expressions of concern with poverty.

14

The anti-poverty dollar

E A C H year, a large sum is spent to prevent or alleviate poverty and poverty-producing conditions. This is the "anti-poverty dollar," by whose size and make-up the extent of society's effort to deal with poverty is measured.

Figure 6 presents the New School study staff's estimate of the total amount spent in this way by public and private agencies in the United States in 1960 to prevent or alleviate poverty. This total anti-poverty expenditure of $52.4 billion represented a little over 10 per cent of the gross national product of $502.6 billion.

FIGURE 6   Estimated Anti-poverty Expenditures, 1960

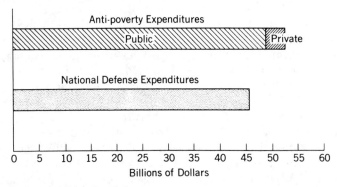

Source: Tables 3 and 4.

Doing away with poverty inevitably requires changing the distribution of income. All of the $52.4 billion represented in this chart was taken from people in the form of taxes or voluntary contributions. To the extent that the taxes or contributions were used for the direct benefit of other people, the money was redistributed.

Programs of palliation such as Aid to Dependent Children and Old Age Assistance represent income redistribution in its most obvious aspect; that is, those who can best afford to pay taxes pay the relief costs

100

of those who pay the least taxes. Those who work help support those
who do not or cannot work and those who are underemployed. Even
public education, among the more palatable types of poverty prevention,
represents a redistribution of income. Taxpayers who have no children
or who have already educated their children, or who send their children
to private schools must pay to help send other people's children, including the children of the poor, to school. Taxes themselves are, of
course, redistributive so long as the taxpayer does not get equal value
in return for the amount he has paid. So practically all public programs
that cost money involve a redistribution of income.

The most palatable anti-poverty program, of course, would be one
that encouraged people with low income to improve their status through
their own effort. This might be done with least pain to other groups by
increased productivity, in which low-income groups might be direct
beneficiaries. Even here, relative income shares might be shifted to
the disadvantage of other groups.

The $52.4 billion in public and private expenditures shown in Fig-
ure 6, which was not much less than the U.S. defense budget, would
seem to indicate that the American people have already assumed a
very large anti-poverty burden. Even if we except Social Security
benefits, which are to some degree financed by their own prospective
recipients, the sum is large.

Related Concepts

Inasmuch as notions similar to the New School's "anti-poverty
dollar" have been set forth, to avoid confusion it is useful to distinguish this concept from the others in detail.

(1) An aggregate of social welfare expenditures, the "social welfare dollar," describes expenditures aimed at reducing "financial un-
certainties associated with old age, premature death, unemployment,
accidental injury and sickness, and substandard conditions.[1] Here
the boundaries of the concept are those of various federal-state Social
Security programs. In its conceptual make-up, the social welfare dollar is not equivalent to the anti-poverty dollar, but the two concepts
overlap.

(2) Every year certain public expenditures meet "social wants,"
defined as those in which the "individual consumer's satisfaction is independent of his own contribution," and for which "true preference

1. John G. Turnbull et al., Economic and Social Security, Ronald Press,
New York, 1962, p. 30.

scales"[1] are unknown. Among such expenditures are payments for
the judiciary system, flood control, sanitary campaigns, and the fight
against venereal disease. Expenditures on social wants are more em-
bracing than the anti-poverty dollar and express a different system of
value judgments and priorities.

(3) "Merit wants" are those "that are satisfied by the market
within the limits of effective demand ... and /which/ become public
wants if considered so 'meritorious' that their satisfaction is provided for through the public budget, over and above what is provided
for through the market and paid for by private buyers."[2] Subsidized
middle-income or low-cost housing, free education, school lunches,
belong to this category. Again, there is much conceptual overlap.
The anti-poverty dollar covers low-income housing subsidies, but to
the extent that middle-income housing subsidies are a cost to the public, they are excluded. Similarly, free education up to grade twelve
is part of the anti-poverty dollar, but a free college education is not.

(4) There are also "remedial expenditures," which are those
"undertaken to meet adverse changes in environment,"[3] where such
changes are due to exogenous factors of demand or to changes in the
production process. The anti-poverty dollar is a form of remedial
expenditure but it does not cover all remedial expenditures. It aims,
for instance, to offset changes in the production process that pull individuals and groups into the poverty band. The anti-poverty dollar,
however, also goes beyond the remedial; for example, it may include
expenditures to individuals and groups that have always been completely
outside the production process.

Discussion of the federal government's "War on Poverty" has
brought out other measures of U. S. society's effort to fight poverty.
These generally have failed to distinguish as to the purpose of the expenditure, and have often either measured the total spent on social
welfare or more simply included most governmental activities of a
domestic nature.

Federal anti-poverty programs introduced in 1963 in Congress in
connection with the hearings on the Economic Opportunity Act of 1964
totaled over $31 billion. In this particular count, the total included
the extension services of the Department of Agriculture as well as di-

1. Richard A. Musgrave, Theory of Public Finance, McGraw-Hill, New York,
1959, pp. 9, 10.

2. Ibid., p. 13.

3. Ibid., p. 189.

rect loans to farmers and funds spent on rural housing repairs. We
have not included any of these items in our anti-poverty measure as
they benefit almost exclusively farmers who are well off. Similarly
included in the measure of "federal programs currently operating to
combat poverty" were items relating to forestry and soil conservation,
public library services and construction, the National Defense Education Act, urban renewal, mortgage insurance, the Department of the
Interior's Geological Survey, the Bureau of Reclamation, the National
Park Service, the Fish and Wildlife Service, and so on—all of which
are excluded from our measure. [1]

1. See House Report No. 1458, 88th Cong., 2nd sess., Economic Opportunity
Act of 1964, June 3, 1964, H.R. 11377, pp. 86-89; and Economic Opportunity Act
of 1964, PL 88-452.

15

The public anti-poverty dollar

T H E New School poverty study staff estimated public expenditures in the fiscal year 1960 to prevent or alleviate poverty at nearly $49 billion, as set out in Table 3. This sum includes both administrative expenses and benefits meted out in cash or in kind. Contrasted to this nearly $49 billion in public expenditures in 1960 was a considerably smaller private anti-poverty expenditure, analyzed in the next section.

The first column in Table 3 lists expenditures aimed at reducing the probability of being poor at some future time. These expenditures, which amount to three-quarters of the total public expenditure for the prevention of poverty, are related to old age, sickness, and disability, to a female being the head of the family, to low education, non-white race, and unemployment. The other one-quarter of the public anti-poverty dollar is made up of costs incurred to alleviate the condition of those who, as recipients of public aid, have been officially declared "poor." These expenditures have been labeled "support" and appear in the second column of the table. Public costs of supporting persons who have not officially been declared poor are included in the fourth column; they are very largely payments under veterans' programs.

A separate counting of benefits actually paid out in cash and in kind in 1960 through public channels to persons who were poor and to persons who would be poor without such income is provided in Appendix 34. Only that part of the public anti-poverty dollar which goes directly to the actually or potentially poor is included in Appendix 34. Instead of measuring society's anti-poverty effort, the total of approximately $29 billion in that table measures what society actually gives families or individuals. The difference between it and the total in Table 3 may be loosely viewed as the measure of the success of the anti-poverty effort. Indeed a fully successful anti-poverty effort would do away with precisely that condition which leads the public authorities to make continued payments to those it continues to call poor. The very essence of an anti-poverty program is the removal of conditions that

TABLE 3 Estimated Public Expenditures to Prevent or Alleviate Poverty, Fiscal Year, 1960 (Millions)

Characteristic	Prevention of Poverty	Support of the Poor	Subtotal	Support of Those Not Officially Declared Poor	Total
Old Age	$10,570.5	$2,170.1	$12,740.6	$ 46.6	$12,787.2
Sickness	2,388.0	2,471.8	4,859.8	453.1	5,312.9
Physical Disability	3,513.3	1,561.4	5,074.7	1,630.8	6,705.5
Absence of Breadwinner	3,721.7	1,360.3	5,082.0	367.0	5,449.0
Unemployment	2,765.7	-------	2,765.7	-------	2,765.7
Substandard Wages	14.9	-------	14.9	-------	14.9
Lack of Skill	242.0	-------	242.0	-------	242.0
Substandard Education	14,358.5	-------	14,358.5	-------	14,358.5
Non-white	0.7	-------	0.7	-------	0.7
Other	--------	1,189.0	1,189.0	-------	1,189.0
Total	$37,575.3	$8,752.6	$46,327.9	$2,497.5	$48,825.4

Source: Col. 1 from Appendix 32; cols. 2 and 4 from Appendix 33. The coverage of each classification, indicated briefly below, is set down in detail in the source tables, and the basis of selection is explained in Appendix 31.

Old-age: Programs classified as preventive include various federal, state, and local pension programs. Supportive measures include Old Age Assistance and medical care and public housing programs for the elderly. Amounts listed in col. 4 represent principally veterans' benefits for which no means test is required.

Sickness: Preventive programs include estimated public expenditures for medical research, medical facilities, school health, maternal and child care, temporary disability insurance, Railroad Retirement Fund programs, school lunch program, environmental health, and narcotics control. Supportive programs include expenditures for public and veterans' hospitals. Other programs are veterans' programs that require no means test.

Disability: Preventive programs include accident prevention, workmen's compensation, vocational rehabilitation, and various types of disability insurance. Supportive programs include Aid to the Permanently and Totally Disabled, Aid to the Blind, veterans' domiciliary care, and veterans' disability pensions.

Absence of breadwinner: Preventive programs include OASI survivorship benefits, plus other survivorship benefits and child welfare. Supportive programs include veterans' death compensation, aid to families of dependent children, surplus foods, free school lunch, institutional care, general assistance, and public housing.

Unemployment: Preventive programs include unemployment insurance.

Substandard wages: Preventive expenditures are for administration of the U.S. Labor Department's Wage and Hour Division, Bureau of Labor Standards, and its Mexican Farm Labor program.

Lack of skill: Preventive expenditures are for the U.S. Labor Department's Bureau of Apprenticeship and Training and federal, state, and local vocational educational programs.

Substandard education: The large sum listed is for public elementary and secondary education, both current expenditures and construction.

Other: Includes portions of the following programs not segregatable by characteristic: surplus foods, institutional care for dependent persons, free school lunches, general assistance, and public housing.

105

make for poverty. Other forms of making the poor non-poor—for example, the negative income tax—are also needed, but they reflect a very different concern with poverty. They reflect concern with conditions rather than causes. This is not to gainsay that all policy measures and all policy discussion must recognize at all times the continuing need for support programs for certain categories of the poor whose situation is not amenable to basic change. Otherwise, obviously, the more successful the anti-poverty effort (particularly the preventive expenditures), the smaller will be the need for direct public payments to the poor.

The detailed components of expenditure under each characteristic in these tabulations are explained in Appendices 32, 33, and 34. The allocation of specific expenditures to the various rows and columns is clearly judgmental and in many senses incomplete. In Table 3, for example, the $700,000 allocated for prevention of poverty linked to the characteristic non-white understates by far society's effort in this field. Attempts to rectify such understatements illustrate the technical aspects of the problem. From non-comparable data it can be estimated, for instance, that the State of New York's anti-discrimination expenditures amounted in 1960 to about $750,000. (The New York State Commission against Discrimination reported expenditures of $968,214 for fiscal 1961.) One might allocate, in addition, about $6.5 million to this figure to cover expenditures for the fair employment practices commissions of the approximately twenty other states in which such programs exist. One might thus conclude that about $7.5 to $8 million could have been allocated to this activity. This procedure was rejected because of the risk of compounding error and because the other categories of our tables may include understatements of the same type.

Parts of the 1960 budget of $120 million of the Bureau of Indian Affairs have been eliminated from our series either because they have been included elsewhere (under "education," for example) or because they are concerned, not with the anti-poverty effort, but with such things as resource management and road construction. United States Public Health Service funds specifically directed to benefit Indians are included under "sickness."

Anti-poverty expenditures connected with sickness are probably overstated, as they include funds for medical research of a broader intent. They also include certain amounts used for stockpiling public health items necessary to civil defense, which have nothing to do with poverty. Expenditures for health services and hospital construction for the military and their families have, on the other hand, been excluded.

Though our measurement of society's total effort against poverty may be approximate and incomplete, the tables highlight the extremely large expenditures involved. And the data for 1960 are representative of the anti-poverty dollar for most years since 1947. In the main, the fluctuations have been small. This in spite of very real differences in U. S. political and economic philosophy regarding poverty. [1]

1. For attitudinal differences, see Seymour Harris, The Economics of the Political Parties, Macmillan, New York, 1962.

16

The private anti-poverty dollar

CERTAIN private outlays are clearly part of the total anti-poverty effort. What individuals save on their own account for their old age, for the education of their children, for the maintenance of their health and for the safeguarding of their income in case of disease are part of the story. Also included are the considerable sums given annually to private social welfare organizations. Many such private actions are related to governmental actions—to the tax laws, for example, with their allowances for charitable expenditure.

While neither charity nor philanthropy is identical with the private anti-poverty dollar, any study of private anti-poverty effort must start from the estimate of total philanthropic contributions—$8.2 billion in 1960 (Table 4). Less than half of what is donated to philanthropic causes has any connection—and then often remote—to anti-poverty actions or policies. As the same table shows, out of a total of about $8.2 billion, a maximum of $3.6 billion can be counted as the upper limit of private anti-poverty expenditures in 1960.

The estimate was constructed essentially by assuming that expenditures and donations labeled "for health and welfare"—regardless of their specific origin or final use—were aimed at preventing or alleviating poverty, or supporting the poor. Also included were expenditures clearly going for identifiable anti-poverty programs.

The amounts under "health" and "welfare" overstate the monetary contribution. They have been enlarged to capture at least part of the value of non-monetary contributions. There is indeed in the private sector much individual voluntary effort, for which no precise figures are available but which in some way must be accounted for, notably doctors' services and those of volunteer social workers.

Obstacles which hinder accurate estimates of government anti-poverty expenditures are foothills compared to the mountains of difficulties presented by private statistics. On the one hand, monies contributed to the various local United Funds and Community Chests are

The Private Anti-poverty Dollar

TABLE 4   Estimated Private Effort to Prevent or Alleviate Poverty, 1960
(Billions)

Type of Recipient Organization	Estimate of Total Receipts	Estimated Upper Limit of Anti-poverty Expenditures
Religious	$4.2	$ .5[a]
Educational	1.3	.8[b]
Welfare	1.2	1.2
Health	1.0	1.0
Foundations	.3[c]	.1
Others	.2	
Total	$8.2	$3.6

Source: Calculated from data in Giving U.S.A.: A Compilation of Facts Related to American Philanthropy, American Association of Fund-Raising Counsel, Inc., New York, 1962, pp. 7, 9, 28 and 45.

a. Based on per cent of current expenditures identifiable as going to anti-poverty activities.

b. Private expenditures for education are overwhelmingly for higher education and come from endowments. Amount here reflects primarily lump-sum payment from the Ford Foundation for its program of improvement of public school education in depressed urban neighborhoods. See Ford Foundation Annual Report, 1960, p. 28.

c. Only amounts paid into endowment funds.

known to the last penny; on the other, only imprecise estimates are available for religious giving. All figures on donations to churches are estimates. Financial reports from other tax-free organizations are often not available to the public. Nor are the contributions and expenditures of very small or localized charities likely to be known with any degree of accuracy.[1]

Figures on donations for charitable and philanthropic purposes from individual income tax returns show almost 15 per cent divergence in estimates of private giving recorded by donors and by the recipient.[2] Nor is the income of philanthropic organizations equivalent to the contributions they receive; many also have income from fees, investments, and (foundations especially) endowments.

1. F. Emerson Andrews, Philanthropic Giving, Russell Sage Foundation, New York, 1960; Ralph Nelson, "Estimates of Private Giving," Tested Knowledge of Business Cycles, 42nd Annual Report, National Bureau of Economic Research, New York, 1962, p. 59.

2. Nelson, op. cit., p. 58.

17

How private and public efforts interact and overlap

HOW private and public efforts interact and support each other is most apparent today in the field of health, particularly health research. About three-fifths of all medical research is now paid for by government.[1] In recent years private philanthropic expenditures for health care and medical research have been rising much more slowly than those by government.

Table 5 shows the growth in the 1950's of the two types of expenditure. At the beginning of the decade, every $32 of selected government health expenditures was matched by $10 in private philanthropic expenditures; by 1960 the governmental share had risen to $47 for every $10 in private expenditures.

The most dramatic change was in research. In the past, research was almost entirely privately sponsored; now the National Institutes of Health, the research arm of the government, constitute the largest and most rapidly growing program supporting American medical research. Their budget is more than four times the total budgets of the thirty-seven largest private national health agencies.[2]

The growth of governmental spending is not unrelated to the proliferation of private groups. Voluntary fund-raising drives, even those not involved in research, increase public awareness of needs and act as catalysts, creating an environment conducive to increased government expenditures. For instance, when the National Association for Retarded Children was formed in 1953, it publicized the extent of mental retardation and the need for research. By 1960 the organization

---

1. Ida C. Merriam, "Social Welfare Expenditures, 1960-61," Social Security Bulletin, November 1962, pp. 3-13. The estimate is for 1961, but, if anything, would rise slightly with the rise of government expenditures as a whole since then.

2. Wise Giving Bulletin, American Association of Fund-Raising Counsel, Inc., Spring 1962 and Spring 1963.

TABLE 5   Private Philanthropic and Selected Public Expenditures for Health
and Medical Services, 1950, 1955, and 1960[a] (Millions)

Services	1950	1955	1960	Per Cent Change 1950-60	Per Cent Change 1955-60
Public (selected)					
Civilian hospital and medical care	$1,170.0	$1,449.5	$2,116.5	80	46
Medical research[b]	55.0	105.9	460.0	736	334
School health (educational agencies)	30.6	66.3	101.1	230	52
Maternal and child health services	29.8	92.9	139.4	368	50
Medical vocational rehabilitation	7.4	9.2	17.7	139	92
Public assistance vendor medical payments	----	211.9	492.5	---	132
Subtotal	$1,292.8	$1,935.7	$3,327.2	157	72
Private philanthropic	400.0	580.0	700.7	75	21
Total public and private philanthropic	$1,692.8	$2,515.7	$4,027.9	150	60
Private philanthropic as per cent of total	24	23	17		

Source: Based on data in Table 5, Ida C. Merriam, "Social Welfare Expenditures, 1960-61," Social Security Bulletin, November 1962, p. 10.

a. Coverage of some items varies from that in other tables for purposes of obtaining comparability over time. For instance, medical vocational rehabilitation expenditures listed here represent only expenses for that purpose of the vocational rehabilitation program. Medical facilities construction costs, both public and private, are excluded.

b. Figures prior to 1960 include only medical and health-related research identified as such; 1960 includes some funds earmarked for other purposes but used in support of research related to health. Government medical research expenditures of the maternal and child health and vocational rehabilitation programs are not included under research.

had an income of $5.8 million, but it had also directed federal attention to the problems and treatment of retardation with a consequent marked increase in government expenditures.

The interaction between private and public activities is particularly evident in the hospital field, the best symbol of direct daily assistance to the poor. A significant division of responsibility has developed.

Most philanthropic hospitals are today devoted to short-term care. Public hospitals increasingly treat long-term illness, including mental disease. Whereas in 1935 philanthropy paid one-seventh of private hospital care, by 1958 the proportion had fallen to about one-twentieth.[1]

Patients helped by philanthropy are not always the most destitute. Hospital expenses of recipients of public assistance are often paid for by the government. But these payments rarely cover the whole bill, and voluntary hospitals may absorb the difference. Not all of the difference is paid for by deliberate philanthropy; some comes from voluntary services provided by doctors. Some, indeed, may also be said to come today from the involuntary contribution of exploited, low-paid hospital workers.[2]

Construction of non-profit hospitals is also no longer strictly voluntary, inasmuch as today the federal government is a large-scale contributor to construction costs, through the Hill-Burton program. During the first decade and a half of the Hill-Burton Act, voluntary non-profit hospitals received 56 per cent of all federal hospital funds and represented 47 per cent of all projects.[3] Interestingly enough, in 1960, according to an unofficial estimate of the Department of Health, Education, and Welfare, $16 million also came from private sources for the construction costs of publicly owned medical facilities.

Whatever estimate for the private anti-poverty dollar one uses, one fact is certain. In spite of the large private contribution, a relatively small proportion of philanthropic contributions goes to help the poor and relatively little of the support of the poor comes from charity.

New ideas, flexibility, venture capital are useful contributions of private philanthropy. Results from efforts stimulated by private expenditures may, in the long run, be applied to areas from which the greatest anti-poverty gains may come. For the present, however, the largest monetary effort and the most difficult policy problems are handled through the public sector.

1. Eli Ginzberg, "Hospitals and Philanthropy," pp. 73-110, in Philanthropy and Public Policy, Frank Dickinson, ed., Conference on Philanthropy sponsored by the National Bureau of Economic Research and Merrill Center for Economics, New York, 1962.

2. To the extent that doctors, for instance, finance their "free" charitable activities by deliberately overcharging well-to-do patients, the well-to-do are in fact carrying part of the burden. A full calculation of involuntary contributions to the private anti-poverty effort would also have to include the relatively low wages paid in other anti-poverty activities. The low wages of teachers and social workers in some of the states might properly be added.

3. Hill-Burton Program: Progress Report, July 1, 1947–June 30, 1961, Public Health Service, U.S. Department of Health, Education, and Welfare, No. 380, 1961, p. 4.

18

How much do the poor pay
for their own support?

THE ANTI-POVERTY contributions of those who were themselves
within the 1960 poverty band cannot be fully isolated.

Public funds used to help the poor and help eliminate poverty com-
posed approximately 44 per cent of the total tax revenues in 1960. The
social insurance component of the anti-poverty dollar at all levels of
government made up, according to our calculations, about one-half of
the total. The rest was financed through general revenues not easily
allocated by income class. [1] To the extent that state and local governments are financed by sales and excise taxes, the tax impact is relatively heavy on low income groups. To the extent that federal income
taxes reflect a progressive bias, federal taxes impose a somewhat
lesser burden on the lower income groups.

Estimates made by the New School poverty study staff indicate
that a larger proportion of the total anti-poverty tax burden is carried
by those earning under $4,000 than by any other income class. Their
burden is out of proportion to this group's incidence in the population.
Figuring on the basis that about half of the public anti-poverty dollar
is social insurance and that income groups below $4,000 pay 23.1 per
cent of that while they pay 12.1 per cent of all taxes other than social
insurance, we arrive at a total of $8.6 billion, or about 18 per cent of
the total, contributed in 1960 by groups with incomes below $4,000. [2]

1. Tax revenues of state and local governments have remained a relatively
stable proportion of total tax revenues. They moved from 30.9 per cent in 1958
to 31.9 per cent in 1960. See Statistical Abstract of the United States, 1962,
Table 543, p. 416.

2. Calculations based on Tax Foundation, Inc., Allocation of the Tax Burden
by Income Class, Project Note No. 45, New York, 1960. One-half of all prop-
erty taxes were allocated on the basis of consumption expenditures, the other
half in line with housing expenditure patterns. Social insurance contributions of
employers were assumed to be passed on to the consumer, and expenditure patterns were used to allocate them. Worker contributions were allocated in ac-
cordance with the distribution of covered earnings. Of all federal and state

Adding to this $8.6 billion a minimum of one-half billion dollars con-
tributed by these income groups to the private anti-poverty dollar
makes for a total of $9.1 billion which the poor contributed to their
own support via government and other agencies in 1960.

---

taxes paid by all groups, 13.7 per cent are social insurance taxes, compared
with 23.3 per cent of all taxes paid by income groups below $4,000 and 3.9 per
cent of taxes paid by the over $15,000 class.

19

Public assistance programs

P U B L I C assistance or "relief" in the United States is channeled
through six major programs of direct financial aid. Five programs
that are financed by matching federal and state funds are known as
"categorical assistance": poverty related specifically to old age (Old
Age Assistance), medical indigence in old age (Medical Assistance for
the Aged), the dependency of childhood (Aid to Dependent Children),
blindness (Aid to the Blind), or a permanent and total disability (Aid to
the Permanently and Totally Disabled). The sixth type of program, totally dependent upon state or local financing, "general assistance," is
also sometimes known as "home relief."

All public assistance programs are anti-poverty programs that
dole out funds only to those whom society administratively defines as
poor. All of these programs are linked to a means test of one kind or
another. The level of aid depends upon the degree to which recipients
would otherwise live below subsistence minima.

In public usage, the term "Social Security" applies only to Old Age,
Survivors, and Disability Insurance; historically and legally, however,
joint federal-state public assistance programs derive from the Social
Security Act of 1935. The 1935 legislation recognized three categorical problems for which assistance programs were established: Old Age
Assistance, Aid to Dependent Children, and Aid to the Blind. The other
two categories, Aid to the Permanently and Totally Disabled and Medical Assistance for the Aged, were recognized later without change in
the essential pattern of support.

Coverage of the five categorical programs has changed with the
number of potential beneficiaries of these programs, society's notions
of need, administrative rulings, and available funds. Of the vast shifts
in the various relief programs since 1936, the most dramatic have
been, first, the very sharp decline in the number receiving locally financed general assistance—reflecting transfer of general assistance
cases into categorical programs such as Aid to the Permanently and Totally Disabled, the general rise in employment, the development of old-
age pensions, and the extension of unemployment insurance benefits—

and, second, the rise in the number of recipients of federal-state financed Aid to Dependent Children.

The poverty of childhood, one of the less well known aspects of the
post-World War II "baby boom," is a rapidly increasing fact of American life. Between 1947 and 1960 the number of recipients (children and
parents) of Aid to Dependent Children tripled.[1] In 1960, the number of
dependent children under 18 benefiting by this program (2,330,000) almost equaled the number aged 65 or over who were completely dependent on Old Age Assistance (2,353,000), though an additional 685,000
aged received such payments to supplement inadequate OASDI checks.[2]
More individual lives are touched by the Aid to Dependent Children program than by Old Age Assistance, Aid to the Permanently and Totally
Disabled, and Aid to the Blind combined. If shifts in the coverage of
the Aid to Dependent Children program are startling, the growth of
average payments is much less so. While this program paid out 92 per
cent more in 1960 than in 1950, the increase in average monthly payments per recipient was 43 per cent. By contrast, average monthly
payments under the Aid to the Blind program and under Old Age Assistance rose by 55 per cent in the 1950-1960 decade.[3] The statistics
made available in the federal reports relate to current dollars. They
therefore suggest a far greater improvement than actually occurred.
When average monthly payments are recomputed in constant dollars—
in real terms—the improvement is much smaller—about 15 per cent
in the first case and 20 per cent in the second.

The original aim of Aid to Dependent Children was to enable wid-
owed mothers to maintain adequate homes for their children; recipients
of such aid now increasingly come from homes broken by divorce, sepa-
ration, or desertion or headed by an unmarried mother.[4] The proportional decrease in coverage of children whose father is dead or incapacitated is not entirely due to changes in the structure of the family.
Many are now receiving aid under Old Age, Survivors, and Disability

1. Historical Statistics of the United States Colonial Times to 1957, U.S.
Bureau of the Census, Series H 186-198, p. 200; Statistical Abstract of the
United States, 1964, Table 413, p. 304.

2. Trend Report, Graphic Presentation, U.S. Department of Health, Education, and Welfare, Bureau of Public Assistance, 1960, pp. 68-69.

3. Statistical Abstract of the United States, 1964, loc. cit.

4. See Trend Report, op. cit., p. 69.

Insurance. Their number increased from 54,000 in 1940 to 1.9 million in 1960.[1] OASDI will increasingly cover these groups.

Along with the "baby boom" has come an increase in the number of the aged. The fact that 14 per cent of all those 65 and over in 1960 were completely dependent on Old Age Assistance relief shows that Social Security, Railroad Retirement, civil service retirement, and private pension plans are far from universal or adequate. The impact of these programs is nevertheless very large and without them the Old Age Assistance program would have to be much larger. It is in fact a declining program, in relation to the size of the aged population. The proportion of aged on Old Age Assistance in 1950, for example, was close to 23 per cent.

Aid to the Permanently and Totally Disabled depends on severe disability; however, a greater number of disabled workers have qualified for disability benefits under OASDI since passage of the 1960 amendment removing the age minimum of 50 years, and the 1958 amendment granting dependents of disabled workers the same benefits as dependents of retired workers.[2]

---

1. Based on Table 60, p. 52, Social Security Bulletin, Annual Statistical Supplement, 1960.

2. Ibid., pp. 98 and 99.

20

Social insurance programs

SINCE 1900, two terms and two related notions, the reduction of "risk" and the establishment of minimum "security," have been central in public discussions of poverty. Both assume that the industrial society brings, along with its advantages, the risk of impoverishment for some. As being poor was viewed in early twentieth century America as the result of inherent insecurities in the market system, the quest for security became the goal of social insurance systems meant to provide support to victims of the vagaries of industrial society. [1] Significantly, U.S. social security legislation has reflected dissatisfaction with the poor relief laws.

As one writer puts it: "Whether by design or by accident, social insurance in the United States has been set up in such a way as to remove it from the controversy of redistribution."[2] The social insurance system of the United States was conceived as an insurance fund in which the beneficiaries take out, in part, what they put in. Elements of redistribution are, indeed, built into the system by the setting of minimum benefits paid irrespective of the level of contributions. This differentiates the system from straight insurance, and, to a degree, favors those whose lifetime earnings have been extremely low. The system is based on the idea that an individual worker's income is to be redistributed over periods in which he does not earn as well as over those in which he does earn, and that the loss of wages which he may incur should determine the benefits he is to receive. Thus it is a system deeply intermeshed with the market and with participation in it.

The major policy debates of the 1950's and 1960's have centered on coverage and the level of benefits of the various insurance systems.

1. Note, for instance, the eloquent and able plea to help the poor through multiple and universal social insurance systems in I.M. Rubinow, The Quest for Security, Henry Holt and Co., New York, 1934.

2. Valdemar Carlson, Economic Security in the United States, McGraw-Hill, New York, 1962, pp. 193-94.

This is still the essence of the debate about minimum wages, unemployment insurance, and the other parts of the social insurance system. Of the major social insurance components, Old Age, Survivors, and Disability Insurance presents the brightest picture. In future years, because of extension in the system's coverage—it now covers almost 95 per cent of all employees and self-employed persons—the proportion of those over age 65 receiving payments will grow significantly. Yet those with extremely limited labor force participation will still be excluded. In spite of extensions over time in OASDI coverage, what does take place as concerns the poverty question is primarily the redistribution of the income of those within the poverty band. The increase in the wage base of OASDI contributions from $4,200 per year to $5,200 gave the OASDI system a slightly greater redistributive impact within the low-income group, which future increases will reinforce.

It is clear that economic insecurity does not tell the whole story of poverty; the social insurance system cannot be appraised in terms of its successes in doing away with poverty as it is not primarily meant to do so. It attacks poverty only to the extent to which the poor are labor market participants. The bulk of the benefits go to those with the greatest participation in the labor market. Our way of life channels minorities into traditional and declining occupations. What is needed is social and administrative ground rules which establish how the society lives and adjustment of these rules to the productive capacity of the nation.

Concentration on the problem of risk and security helps explain why, until recently, despite the considerable U. S. anti-poverty expenditure, no anti-poverty policy, as such, existed. Most discussions of social welfare have bypassed entirely the actual problem posed by contemporary "class" poverty. The public effort was designed primarily to cope with the aberrations of the economic system, not to bring the abject poor into the system.

Debate on whether the war on poverty can best be waged by pursuing a full employment policy or by selective spending on other activities misses the mark. The great economic growth of the last decade and a half has made no significant dent in the "class" characteristics of abject poverty except to alleviate somewhat the poverty of the aged.

21

The feasibility of preventing poverty

IF POVERTY is defined in static terms, as in the President's annual economic report, an increasing rate of economic growth will obviously reduce poverty—eventually. With poverty defined in contemporary terms, as in this study, the matter is more complex. We have
noted at each period the existence of circularity between accustomed
styles of life and budget criteria. What does this mean to us today,
as we talk about eliminating poverty? As living standards in general
rise, including standards at the lowest end of the poverty band—for
recipients of relief—we might ask: Are we not making the eradication
of "poverty" impossible by continually jacking up the standards?

The answer to this question is clearly no. It is no for the reason
that the definition of poverty in each generation represents not only
the contemporary life style of the low income classes; it also represents a life style below which society agrees—in terms of dollars—
that its citizens should not be allowed to fall. Definitions of poverty
therefore reflect not only habitual expenditure at the poverty band level;
they reflect current social ideals. If people are complacent about the
living conditions of those within the poverty band, standards will not
change much. If public opinion discerns great inequities in life styles
on the poverty level, standards may improve. The test is whether people are willing to pay what it costs. Relief budgets and the other budgets in the poverty band—"minimum adequacy" and "minimum comfort"
budgets—tell a great deal about U.S. ideals as well as the realities of
life at low income levels.

Considering poverty for a moment in terms of inequality rather
than insufficiency, anyone willing to look at the Statistical Abstract of
the United States can readily see that the lowest 20 per cent of the population gets only about 5 per cent of the national income—and that their
share has fallen slightly in recent years. Some such inequity will always exist—whether the lowest 20 per cent gets 5 per cent or 4 per
cent or 6 per cent or whatever. In this sense, poverty is indeed eter-

nal, just as physical and mental qualities are unequal, and hereditary advantages are usually unequal. If total national income rises, the proportion received by the bottom 20 per cent might very well remain at 5 per cent; but in terms of this study, poverty could conceivably be eliminated if the increase sufficed to bring every family and every individual in the bottom 20 per cent up to what society currently accepts as minimal standards.

There is another inequity: certain groups have become disproportionately and increasingly the primary victims of poverty. The statistical odds are clearly against them—non-whites, the young, the old, single people, female heads of families, rural farm families, southern families, residents of depressed areas. To the extent that current social ideals accept the notion that a little poverty is all right, so long as it happens to members—or even to most members—of certain groups, it reflects indifference. It may even reflect hypocrisy in people who with the next breath insist that America is a land of equal opportunity, that any man of ability can rise on his own.

Be that as it may, we shall in this discussion consider only the question whether we can afford to bring those at the lower end of the poverty band up to levels presently considered as minimal.

Requirements for significant economic growth in terms of resources are far greater than is generally assumed. In his analysis of past trends in the U.S. economy, Denison arrived at the conclusion that to permanently raise the rate of growth of national income by one per cent (from 3 per cent annually to 4 per cent) within one year would require an increase in net capital formation from $25 billion to something between $65 and $85 billion annually, or about three times the present net investment.[1] To increase net investment from private sources by $40 to $60 billion a year seems a sheer impossibility within the present institutional framework. A great stride toward a substantially higher rate of growth seems, under these circumstances, far from immediately obtainable. Even deficit spending to achieve such a rate of investment could obtain a rate of growth at best corresponding to the level of full employment and full utilization of capacity.

If the solution of the problem of poverty in an affluent society through a substantial increase in the growth rate seems to encounter serious obstacles, the question of redistribution of incomes must be tackled directly.

1. Edward Denison, The Sources of Economic Growth, Committee for Economic Development, Supplementary Paper No. 13, New York, January 1962, p. 163.

The Arithmetic of Redistribution

What is the ability of our economy to do away with poverty with
existing resources through the redistribution of available income?
Seeking to answer this question, the poverty study staff calculated the
amount of money that would be required in order to bring the income
of those below the three levels of need specified in this study up to
those income levels while providing the rest of the population a "minimum comfort" income.

The method used is explained in Appendix 35. Briefly, the amount
of disposable personal income available for redistribution was obtained
by subtracting (1) the income already received by the poor and (2) the
amount required to provide the non-poor with the highest level, that of
"minimum comfort." The residual was considered as a potential fund
for redistribution and the income required to eliminate poverty was
taken as a percentage of this fund.

From Appendix 35 it will be seen that $163.5 billion of the $351.8
billion of disposable personal income in 1960 would have had to be set
aside to guarantee all those above the "minimum comfort" income level
a "comfort" standard of income. Table A of that appendix shows that,
after allowing for this guarantee and for the amount already received
by families and unattached individuals whose income was less than the
1960 "minimum comfort" standard, there remained $120.5 billion of
disposable personal income available for redistribution. Since $41.9
billion would have been required to be added to the income of those below "minimum comfort" in order to bring them up to that standard, a
redistribution of more than one-third of the $120.5 billion would have
been necessary to assure "minimum comfort" for all in 1960. Such a
redistribution would undoubtedly not be politically feasible. By contrast, if 1929 standards of "minimum comfort" were the goal sought,
it could have been achieved for all in 1960 by utilizing only 4.1 per
cent of the disposable personal income available for redistribution.

By 1960 standards of "minimum adequacy" the potential fund for
redistribution was $153.3 billion—again after deducting the "guarantee"
of $163.5 billion for those above the "minimum comfort" level and the
amount already received by those below the "adequacy" level. Of this
$153.3 billion, $20.9 billion, or 13.6 per cent, would have had to be
redistributed in order to assure that nobody fell below the "adequacy"
standard of income. Whether an additional redistribution of 13.6 per
cent would call for substantial changes in the structure of society or
not is a matter of judgment. It too would probably occasion violent op-
position.

Moving from an "adequacy" standard to the elimination of abject
poverty, so that nobody would be below the 1960 "subsistence" income

level and everybody above the "minimum comfort" level would still be guaranteed a "comfort" standard of income, we see that a much smaller additional income redistribution would have been needed—less than 3 per cent.

That the economy is affluent is clear; that it is not affluent enough, in its current performance, to provide everybody with what contemporary society deems minimally comfortable is also clear. At the level of "adequacy" the problem is more complex. Here the exercise with the arithmetic of income redistribution does not provide sufficient guidance, or even if a "once-over" redistribution of 13.6 per cent were feasible, it could not easily be repeated. To bring the poor below this level to current standards of "minimum adequacy," a host of long-range policies, depending heavily for their implementation on higher economic growth rates and significant secular changes in income, would be required. But at the level of "subsistence" current affluence is sufficient and the existing structure of incomes no impediment. A redistribution of 3 per cent or less—amounting in 1960 to $4.6 billion and representing a rise of less than 10 per cent in public anti-poverty expenditures—would appear to be not only feasible but easy.

Policy implications

A S N O T E D earlier, it was not the purpose of the New School poverty study to present a specific program, but to define and delineate the problem and to set forth broad guidelines.

Poverty, it has been seen, is a matter of both insufficiency and inequality. These concepts, while they have been defined objectively, in terms of budgets based on what Americans at various income levels customarily have had at each period, reflect in fact a changing climate of opinion over the years as to what even the poorest Americans might reasonably expect to have. In the future as in the past, the final determination of what society must do will be made in terms of what level of living the United States "ought" to consider minimal in terms of current possibilities and expectations. In addition, it will now have to be made in new terms—whether a self-professing "open society" can tolerate, not the existence of income differentials, but the existence of income differentials on the basis of social and demographic "classes."

A large number of the abject poor and some of those living below a standard of "minimum adequacy" receive part of their income, in money or in kind, from anti-poverty programs. These transfers provide a form of redistribution. To it the support of family members and gifts must be added because these contribute a large part of the income of the poor. Charitable anti-poverty contributions represent voluntary redistribution.

The redistributive effect is temporary when—as in the case of food distributions—it only fills the gap between immediate needs and consumable resources. It is permanent—as in the case of medical services, when the service re-establishes and enriches the individual's earning power—and when, assuming employment is available—the individual is returned to employment in which he earns enough to extricate himself from a temporary condition.

To the extent that the recipients of anti-poverty benefits are already potentially upward-moving socially and economically, the benefit may provide the needed push to make them move again. Unemployment insurance, for instance, may work this way. Other payments protecting the individual from income interruptions in today's industrial society may also be redistributive.

The bulk of today's poor, however, are <u>not</u> on an upward escalator: they are <u>not</u> poor because of temporary interruptions in the workings of the economy, but because they are <u>outside</u> the economy. Schemes such as unemployment insurance are effective only if they involve individuals whose skills have not been eliminated, or individuals who are transferrable within the framework of production. Counseling, retraining, and labor market reorganization are also needed as anti-poverty devices. The bulk of supposed "anti-poverty" expenditures are not redistributive. To the extent that they are supportive rather than preventive, they do not lead to increased access to income. They fail to improve the individual's capacities, his assets, his ability to earn.

The reason is simple. Most anti-poverty measures existing or proposed until late 1963 centered on Social Security programs; and as such programs involve only those who have jobs in covered industries, they largely exclude the abject poor. A true anti-poverty campaign would concentrate on those who are virtually outside the economy. The new efforts of the Office of Economic Opportunity are of this type.

We have shown that the poverty population of the United States in the 1960's is characterized by specific socio-demographic attributes. Families that are aged or rural farm or non-white or headed by a female, or that have some or all of these characteristics in combination, account for 70 per cent of the abject poor. In absolute terms, the largest group within the poverty band are those families possessing only one such characteristic. However, the most severe poverty exists among families with more than one of these poverty-linked attributes. This was shown earlier in Section 5, where the details of the New School study on the convergence of poverty-linked characteristics were briefly reported. Here the policy implications of those findings can be discussed in a general manner.

In terms of convergence poverty is a matter of social structure and from this comes the requirement that policy be oriented toward special groups. Action to improve the conditions of families with several poverty-linked characteristics must clearly precede that aimed at helping families with fewer of these characteristics. But how does one go about doing so? Obviously relief can be provided for families with multiple poverty-linked characteristics. But if one is to move against the very conditions that create poverty, a new and more basic question arises. How does one go about establishing priorities in selecting the characteristics that need to be done away with to bring about the greatest possible reduction in poverty?

The New School poverty study staff has tried to answer this question by analyzing costs and yields of existing and contemplated programs.

These studies are too technical and the results too ephemeral to be reported here. On the other hand, what is worthwhile noting is the result of a simple selective disaggregation of the statistics on convergence presented in Appendix 10 and Appendix 11.

The technique used was the simple subtraction of one poverty-linked characteristic at a time and a comparison of the results. Table 6 measures the income effect of removing one poverty-linked charac-

TABLE   6   Effect of Removing One of Three Poverty-Linked Characteristics
(Change in percentage of families below the subsistence level)

Characteristic(s) of Family Head	Per Cent Below "Subsistence" Level	Characteristic(s) of Family Head	Per Cent Below "Subsistence" Level
Non-white, Rural farm, Female		Non-white, Rural farm, Aged	
	86.6		81.1
minus:		minus:	
non-white=	54.8	non-white=	54.9
rural farm=	64.6	rural farm=	62.6
female=	78.3	aged=	78.3
Non-white, Aged, Female		Aged, Rural farm, Female	
	67.5		52.5
minus:		minus:	
non-white=	37.2	rural farm=	37.2
aged=	64.6	aged=	54.8
female=	62.6	female=	54.9

Source: Appendix 10.

teristic from the population of families with three such characteristics. The table shows that the removal of the characteristic non-white reduces the percentage of families below subsistence to a greater degree than the removal of the characteristic rural farm. The effect is least marked in terms of removing any third characteristic from families with rural farm as one of their three poverty-linked characteristics. Table 7 shows, in a similar manner, the effect of removing one poverty-linked characteristic from families with two. The pattern that emerges from these tables throws some light on the success of past policy concerning the aged. In two instances we find that subtracting the aged has a modifying rather than a depressing effect on the percentage of extremely low income units. Rural farm families headed by aged females

TABLE 7   Effect of Removing One of Two Poverty-Linked Characteristics
(Change in percentage of families below the subsistence level)

Characteristic(s) of Family Head	Per Cent Below "Subsistence" Level	Characteristic(s) of Family Head	Per Cent Below "Subsistence" Level
Non-white, Rural farm	78.3	Non-white, Female	64.6
minus:		minus:	
rural farm=	28.6	female=	28.6
non-white=	34.5	non-white=	38.0
Non-white, Aged	62.6	Rural farm, Aged	54.9
minus:		minus:	
aged=	28.6	aged=	34.5
non-white=	39.6	rural farm=	39.6
Rural farm, Female	54.8	Aged, Female	37.2
minus:		minus:	
female=	34.5	aged=	38.0
rural farm=	38.0	female=	39.6

Source: Appendix 10.

were slightly better off than rural farm families headed by non-aged
females. Age is the one area where, adequate or not, there does exist a national policy and program of insurance. Removing the non-
white characteristic helps here too, but less so.

The reduction of the impact on poverty of certain characteristics
cannot be done by fiat. It takes a multitude of programs and many actions by many institutions. The many actions required to do away with
poverty must support each other. For instance, while it is recognized
that expansion of employment is a prerequisite of doing away with poverty among Negroes, the fact that Negroes have lesser educational opportunities and, for a number of reasons, take less advantage of them
assures us that expansion of employment alone will not do away with
poverty in this group.

Policy priorities need to be set up in full recognition of the extent
of class unemployment and related poverty, in the recognition of affluence and of poverty. The primacy of class unemployment calls for action along a variety of lines related to education, training, and retrain-

ing within the local, state, federal, and private systems. More effective labor market organization is required, and the upgrading of employment and counseling services. The changing of prejudicial hiring practices and action against discrimination are obvious prerequisites. Apprenticeship training and, in some of its aspects, collective bargaining also call for modification.

Private industry and organized labor can agree to lower hiring requirements to help provide jobs for those with little training. Many job requirements, especially in service industries, are unrealistically high, effectively shutting out the abject poor. Special joint union-management manpower training programs could cushion the impact of technological change and—in a small way—facilitate the introduction of some of the poor into society. Discrimination against individuals by employers on the basis of color or age or sex requires a wide range of actions. In the case of age discrimination, for instance, employers might be given tax relief for the increased pension and insurance expenditures that might follow from hiring older workers. Raising the maximum subject to payroll tax for Social Security to, say, $9,000 would provide better old-age pensions.

Beyond educational and social insurance programs, U.S. society has mostly paid lip service to the idea of true poverty prevention. Public services are neglected in favor of concentration on the market aspects of the problem. Human beings, too, are social assets and worthy of attention. It is now widely accepted that differences in the rate of economic development of various societies can be explained as much by different amounts and rates of "investment in human beings" as by investments in capital goods. Such investment in human beings might take one or more of the following forms: educational enrichment programs aimed at the very young children of the poor, adult literacy and retraining programs, specialized training for new entrants to the labor market, national health services financed out of general revenues, fair employment practices legislation, increased emphasis on public housing, and mass investment in the underdeveloped areas of the United States. Extension of minimum-wage coverage could be accomplished without extensive governmental expenditure.

Private welfare agencies can pioneer in formulating new programs. In most cases, private welfare now works with the top of the poverty band and functions in spreading middle-class values. In the future, private welfare agencies should spearhead anti-poverty action at <u>all</u> levels, as does the Ford Foundation in its "Big Cities" programs of enriched education for deprived urban children. Other private groups worthy of emulation include the North Carolina Fund and the Taconic Foundation.

Preventive measures would be fiscally more sound than a continued heavy reliance on palliation. To the extent that they are aimed at removing links between poor health, mental incapacity, substandard education, and lack of skill, they lead to making the poor more productive members of society. Supportive measures alone, indeed, may be the only realistic program for many individuals in poverty-linked groups. To avoid continuing support for another group of 20 million abjectly poor people, however, selective programs might help improve their physical and mental capacities.

It is also necessary to further clarify the relationship of defense expenditures to employment, and to understand full employment policies and economic growth policies as parallel to but separate from anti-poverty measures. Debate on whether the war against poverty can best be waged by pursuing a full employment policy or by selective spending on other activities misses the mark. The great economic growth of the last decade and a half has made no significant dent in the "class" characteristics of abject poverty, except for relatively successful effort alleviating somewhat the poverty of the aged. The significance of rapid economic growth is that the chance of instituting programs is far greater if they are carried out in periods of rapid growth. So viewed, economic growth becomes a necessary, albeit not a sufficient, condition for success. It is important to realize that we can have growth without full employment, full employment without growth, both without significant inroads on poverty, and the elimination of poverty without either. Noting that these developments are separable does not, of course, mean that separate pursuit of each alternative is either desirable or possible. Clearly, full employment and doing away with poverty are both desirable goals.

Certain limitations on poverty policies other than the size of the expenditure limit further action. One problem has roots in traditional U.S. ideas concerning the poor, traceable to the punitive English poor laws of an earlier day and to individualistic social thought. Behind recent controversies over relief funds, such as the demand of some local citizens and authorities that relief recipients work "or else," there is obviously lurking a continuing national antagonism toward the poor. Relief, however, is a necessary if regrettable requirement for a minority of the population. Here all one can do is try to wait for our society to separate those who believe in the value of the individual human personality from those who do not.

Although anti-poverty policies are necessarily linked, as a practical matter, to the gross national product, and specifically to the amount of it needed to prevent poverty, they should not be considered primarily a means of stimulating the nation's production. Present-day affluence makes it possible to do away with poverty. If we do not do so now, there is no way of knowing whether the problem will in the future be equally manageable.

Summary

THE MAJOR conclusions of the New School for Social Research
poverty study can be reduced to the following propositions:

Poverty is a relative term. Who is by general consensus considered
poor differs with time and place—and also by administrative or other
reason for which the judgment is made.

U. S. workers' family budgets prepared since the early 1900's by public and private agencies offer a convenient means of establishing a
rough consensus at various times and places as to who is poor—for
various reasons. The comparative study of workers' budgets since
1900 constitutes a history of a climate of opinion concerning the nature and extent of poverty.

There is a strong factor of circularity in the standards upon which
workers' budgets are based. Not only do they reflect what society
thinks men "ought" to spend for "subsistence," "minimum adequacy,"
or "minimum comfort," but also what contemporary low-income people customarily do spend when they buy what is budgeted for. Workers' family budgets, especially at the "subsistence" level, thus reflect the customary, contemporary life style of the poor, as society
judges it ought to be and as the poor expect it to be.

Society's judgment as to what workers' families "ought" to spend tends
also to reflect the extent of its concern about poverty at any time.

Workers' family budgets offer means to estimate the extent of poverty
at any given time, as the problem is seen to be at the time, when related to the contemporary distribution of income.

Time comparisons concerning poverty made in terms of contemporary
standards give different results from those made in static terms.
When contemporary standards are applied for the years from 1947 to
1960 the proportion of households living below levels of "minimum
adequacy" and "minimum comfort" has not changed very much. The
proportion of households living below "minimum subsistence" has decreased from 15 per cent to 11 per cent.

The present is a period of rising expectations all over the world, and
especially so in the United States. The United States economy, in
terms of its contemporary performance, <u>can</u> do away with poverty
at the budgetary level of "minimum subsistence'.' ($2,660 for a fam-
ily of four in 1960). It is not sufficiently affluent to make every family "minimally comfortable" in terms of the Bureau of Labor Statistics' Interim City Worker's Family Budget of 1959 or recent University of California worker budgets (i. e., again for a family of four in
1960, $5,610).

Living in an affluent society, we are especially aware that the proportionate share of the low income classes in our total national product
is still small, remaining at about the level of the Depression years
of the 1930's. They have benefited in only a token way from the general improvement in living styles; some, being outside the economy
almost entirely, have not benefited at all.

Today's low-income Americans include a disproportionate number from
certain demographic groups. We are developing a new type of poverty—the poverty of "underdog" or "pariah" classes versus the mass
poverty characteristic of our economy during the Depression decade
of the 1930's.

Non-whites, female heads of families, rural families, the very young,
the aged, families with more than six children under 18 years of age,
all have a much greater likelihood of being poor than other members
of the population. Individuals who live alone have also a greater
likelihood of being poor than those who live with their families.

Where families and individuals have not merely one but two or more
of these characteristics the probability of their being poor is much
greater. A large number of those living at or below "minimum subsistence" have more than one of these attributes.

In general these groups with a great likelihood of being poor had a
slightly greater likelihood of poverty in 1960 than in 1947.

The groups with a great likelihood of being poor are also most likely
to be unemployed, underemployed, or ill-paid. The most serious
aspect of the unemployment problem is the growing amount of "structural" unemployment resulting from permanent changes in the job
market. These are due to rising factory mechanization, the decline

in blue-collar jobs relative to the growing number of white-collar jobs—many held by women—and to geographic shifts in industry.

The "underendowment" in personal assets of the contemporary poor— their generally low levels of skill, education, and health—the result of cultural deprivation, is one of the most important aspects of their poverty.

Americans have traditionally considered poverty an aspect of the employment problem. But being entirely outside the economy, many of the abject poor (those below the "subsistence" level) do not benefit by the nation's growing productivity. Consequently, programs aimed at increasing productivity will have little helpful effect on them unless they become productive members of society. To do so they need help in increasing their "personal assets."

Most present-day U.S. anti-poverty programs involve an assumed relationship with the labor market, as do, for instance, unemployment compensation and old-age insurance. In these programs, benefits are roughly proportional to length of employment and level of compensation. Those with a great likelihood of being poor have also histories of low earnings and long-term unemployment and therefore benefit little from such programs.

The United States spends each year large amounts for a variety of social purposes. To measure the effort of the society in fighting poverty the concept of "anti-poverty dollar" was devised. The size of the anti-poverty dollar was found to be impressive, but poverty remained.

A large part of the U.S. anti-poverty expenditure goes for palliation instead of prevention. A restructuring of spending policies with more emphasis on prevention would help obviate the necessity of continued large expenditures for palliation.

The national taxation system reduces the effectiveness of anti-poverty efforts. To a considerable extent, the very low-income individuals who are employed help finance governmental programs that are intended to help them.

The New School study concludes that to deal more effectively with the problem of poverty requires greater investment in human beings as well as in capital goods. Such investment is not only economically sound; it is also morally right.

APPENDICES

LIST OF APPENDICES

Selected Quantity Budgets for Worker Families, 1905–1959

Year	Budget	Purpose	Description
1905	*New York City Working Men (L. B. More— R. Sage Fdn.)	Living wage	"Fair living wage" (A)
1907	*Penn. Mill Workers	Charity	"Working margin" (A)
1908	New York City Working Men (R. C. Chapin)	Charity	"Normal standard" (C)
1908	*Southern Cotton Mill Workers (U.S. Bureau of Labor Statistics	Wage determination	Two separate budgets: "Minimum to maintain physical efficiency" (S) & "Fair" (A)
1914	*Philadelphia Textile Mill (E. L. Little— W. J. H. Cotton)	Living wage	"Fair" (C)
1914	N. Y. Factory Investigating Commission (F. H. Streighthoff)	Living wage— N. Y. State	"Adequacy, decency" (A)
1914	Chicago Stockyards (J. C. Kennedy)	Charity	"Minimum decency" (S)
1915	New York City Charity Assn.	Charity	"Minimum" (S)
1915	New York City, Bureau of Mun. Research	Wage determination, city employees (unskilled)	"Adequate" (A)
1917	*Dallas Wage Commission	Wage determination	Two separate budgets: "Lowest bare existence" (S) & "Safe normal living" (A)
1917	Philadelphia Bureau of Mun. Research	Wage determination, city employees	
1917	New York City (W. S. Gibbs)		"Minimum" (S)

Year	Budget	Purpose	Description
1917	New York City (Bellevue Hospital, M. Wadley)	Typical worker's family	"Decent standard" (S)
1917	Pacific Coast Workers (J. B. Peixotto—Univ. of Calif.)	Wage determination	"Minimum standard of wholesome living" (A)
1917	*Seattle-Tacoma Street Railway Workers (W. F. Ogburn)	Wage determination	"Minimum comfort" (C)
1918	*N. Y. Charity Organization Society	Relief charity	"Minimum" (S)
1918	*National War Labor Board (W. F. Ogburn)	Wage determination	"Minimum subsistence" (A)
1919–1926	Natl. Industrial Conference Board local budget studies: Lawrence, Mass.	Wage determination	"Minimum but reasonable" (A)
1919–1926	*Fall River, Mass. Greenville, S. C. & Charlotte, N. C. N. Hudson Co., N. J. Cincinnati, Ohio Worcester, Mass. Detroit, Mich. Pa. Anthracite Area New York City	Wage determination	"Minimum but reasonable" (A)
1919	*Washington, D. C. Govt. employees (U. S. Bureau of Labor Statistics)	Wage determination	"Health and decency" (C)
1920	Worker's Family (U. S. Bureau of Labor Statistics) Civil Service Workers (revised)	Wage determination	"Health and decency" (C)
1920	U. S. Bituminous Coal Commission (W. F. Ogburn)	Wage determination	"Health and decency" (C)
1921	California Cost of Living Survey (Univ. of Calif.)	Wage determination, state civil service workers	"Minimum health and comfort" (C)
1921	Clerical Workers, New York City (Bureau of Mun. Research)	Wage determination, civil service workers	"Health and decency" (C)

Year	Budget	Purpose	Description
1923	*Univ. of Calif. — Heller Committee for Research in Social Economics—Laborers and Clerks (San Francisco) (regularly revised)	Wage determination	"Minimum comfort" (C)
1923	Eastern Mass. Street Railway Co. employees	Wage determination	"Proper and suitable" (C)
1926-1927	National Industrial Conference Board Twelve Industrial Cities	Wage determination, industrial workers	"Fair American standard" (C)
1927	Locomotive Firemen	Wage determination	"Health and decency!"
1928	The Labor Bureau, Inc. Skilled Workers	Wage determination	"Health and decency" (C)
1934	*New York City Dept. of Public Welfare	Public relief	"Minimum" (S)
1935	*WPA (M. L. Stecker)	Wages, public works	"Emergency" (A)
1938	*U.S. Bureau of Labor Statistics North and South	Cost of living	"Customary" (A)
1939	Pa. Dept. of Public Assistance	Public Assistance	"Standards of Public Assistance" (S)
1942	New York Charity Organization Society	Charity, relative responsibility	"Ordinary necessities" (A)
1944	*Textile Workers, South & New England	Wage determination	"Subsistence" (A)
1946	*City Worker's Family Budget (Bureau of Labor Statistics) (regularly revised)	Wages—inter-city differences	"Health, efficiency, nurture of children, social participation, maintenance of self-respect and the respect of others" (A)
1948	Haynes Foundation, Los Angeles (G. S. Goldberg)	Moderate-income families	
1950	Allegheny Co., Pa., Health and Welfare Federation	Charity—Fee setting and counseling	"Health and decency" (A)

Year	Budget	Purpose	Description
1953	Metropolitan Welfare Council, New York City	Fee setting and counseling	
1955	*Kansas City Council of Social Agencies	Fee setting and counseling	"Adequate" (A)
1955	Welfare and Health Council of New York City	Fee setting and counseling	
1957	Metropolitan Atlanta Community Service, Inc.	Fee setting and counseling	
1957	Public Health Federation, Cincinnati	Fee setting and counseling	
1957	United Community Services, Washington, D. C.		
1958	*Aid to Dependent Children—49 states (U.S. Bureau of Public Assistance survey)	Relief	"Subsistence, decency and health" (W. Va., low; Nevada, high) (S)
1959	*Interim City Worker's Family Budget (U.S. Bureau of Labor Statistics)	Wages—inter-city differences	"Modest but adequate" "Prevailing standards" (C)

*Used in computing the figures presented in Tables A and B of Appendix 2.

Note: Years refer to date of price levels surveyed, not publication dates.

(S) "subsistence" level; (A) "adequacy" level; (C) "comfort" level.

Calculation of the Poverty Band

Budget estimates in Table A indicate the estimated cost of maintaining a family of four (consisting of an employed father, an unemployed mother, and two minor children) at the level of minimum requirements specified in budgets over the years since 1905 of the "minimum subsistence," "minimum adequacy," and "minimum comfort" types. This cost is expressed in <u>current dollars</u>. In Table B the cost is expressed in constant 1960 dollars.

Figures underlined in Table A are taken directly from a specific budget. Where more than one budget was available for a given year and level, or where no budget was available for that year and/or that level, the figure was interpolated.

Where necessary, differently structured budgets were recompiled for a family of this size and composition. For instance, many such budgets in the early 1930's, calculated for a five-person family, were recompiled for comparability in terms of four persons. (Many budgets also exist that make separate tabulations under all budget items for adults by both sex and age and for children of various ages, so that they can be added up for individual families. Separate budgets also exist for single males and females of various ages. A large number of budgets for unmarried females exist; these were prepared starting in the early 1900's in connection with minimum-wage and other protective legislation for women. Other types of budgets exist for retired couples and retired single males and females.)

With two exceptions no budgets which simply applied new prices to previously determined budgets were included. The two exceptions were made in order to obtain comparable figures. The Heller budgets, at the "minimum comfort" level for the years 1920-60, include some that were merely repriced though content was frequently reassessed. The same applies to a set of figures at the "subsistence" level compiled by the Charity Organization Society and the Community Service Society, covering 1918-33, and by the New York Department of Welfare, for 1934 to date. Otherwise all budgets of an authoritative nature, which were guideposts for their period, have been included.

The mid-point of the band, in both Tables A and B, is the average of the three budget levels shown.

Basis of Men's Low Wage Index

Annual earnings for unskilled male labor arrived at by combining hourly earnings with hours worked per year.

In the index, hourly earnings, 1919-60, are for common labor on federal-aid highway projects, and the data were collected by the Bureau of Public Roads (communication from U.S. Department of Commerce 4/4/62). The 1900-1914 estimates are derived from earnings of unskilled labor in manufacturing industries; data on full-time earnings developed by Coombs (Whitney Coombs, The Wages of Unskilled Labor in Manufacturing Industries in the U.S., 1890-1924, Columbia University Press, New York, 1926, p. 99) are divided by average full-time hours per week as developed by Rees (Albert Rees, Real Wages in Manufacturing, 1890-1914, Princeton University Press, Princeton, 1961, p. 33).

Average hours per year per worker for 1909-60 are from Bureau of Labor Statistics data for production workers in manufacturing (Employment and Earnings Statistics, U.S. Department of Labor, Bulletin No. 1312, Washington, D.C., 1961, p. 31). The figures uncover the estimates of working time implicit in other wage series. They reflect average paid-for hours per year. The BLS derived data by taking an annual average of monthly paid-for hours and converting that into annual average hours per week; they were multiplied by 52 to set them on an annual basis. Since the early 1940's, when such "fringes" as vacations and sick leave have become important, unadjusted BLS data—which are paid-for hours, rather than scheduled or standard hours, and relate to all production workers on the payroll—differ considerably from hours actually worked.

The hours data for 1899-1904 are from John W. Kendrick, Productivity Trends in the U.S. (Princeton University Press, Princeton, 1961, p. 455), and are conceptually similar to the BLS data (Kendrick derived his estimates of average paid-for hours from Census of Manufactures data on standard hours; see pages 443-48).

To test for reliability, the series developed here was compared to such other readily available information as seemed relevant. In general, our data appeared reasonable with respect both to level and movement of comparable data.

The earnings rate of common labor was compared with the wage rate for unskilled labor on railroads, computed from Interstate Commerce Commission data by the National Industrial Conference Board, for 1916-48. The two sets of rates, in general, show the same pattern of movement, or only minor divergences. The common-labor

rate varies at the most by 5 per cent from the entrance rate for unskilled labor collected by the Federal Reserve Bank of New York for
1915-20 (cited by Leo Wolman in Recent Economic Changes in the
U.S., Vol. II, Ch. VI, President's Commission on Unemployment,
McGraw-Hill, New York, 1929, p. 437); after 1920 the two series di-
verge.

The 1900-1914 data derived from Coombs were checked against
several other sources. The 1914 earnings rate was found to be slightly below the N.Y. Federal Reserve Bank's rate, an average entrance
rate for the New York district. The estimates for 1900-1909 turned
out to be whole cents' equivalents to low-wage hourly earnings computed from Paul F. Brissenden, Earnings of Factory Workers, 1899
to 1927 (Census Monograph No. 10, Washington, D.C., p. 124). The
index constructed here took the mean of the four lowest (out of thirty-
five industries) nominal hourly rates for each year for male workers,
as estimated by Brissenden.

Note that this index is conceptually different from that computed
by Paul Douglas. His series on average annual earnings for unskilled
labor (Paul Douglas, Real Wages in the U.S., 1890-1926, Houghton
Mifflin, Boston, 1930, p. 477) allowed for layoffs, but not for part-
time or casual work. His series told what the average worker earned,
while ours tells what a worker earned on the average.

TABLE   A   The Poverty Band, 1905-60, in Current Dollars

| | Budget Level | | | |
Year	"Minimum Subsistence"	"Minimum Adequacy"	"Minimum Comfort"	Mid-point of Band
1905	413	625	726	588
1906	413	625	726	588
1907	413	625	726	588
1908	413	625	750	596
1909	438	643	787	623
1910	462	662	820	648
1911	490	685	850	675
1912	517	706	883	702
1913	550	725	916	730
1914	582	750	942	758
1915	620	775	1,050	815
1916	635	855	1,187	892
1917	657	952	1,325	978
1918	829	1,330	1,549	1,236
1919	1,051	1,422	1,887	1,453
1920	1,128	1,486	2,077	1,564
1921	1,007	1,413	1,859	1,426

TABLE A The Poverty Band, 1905-60, in Current Dollars (Continued)

	Budget Level			
Year	"Minimum Subsistence"	"Minimum Adequacy"	"Minimum Comfort"	Mid-point of Band
1922	1,054	1,413	1,837	1,435
1923	1,068	1,450	1,820	1,446
1924	1,083	1,519	1,800	1,467
1925	1,093	1,562	1,775	1,476
1926	1,136	1,600	1,762	1,499
1927	1,136	1,588	1,740	1,488
1928	1,136	1,575	1,714	1,475
1929	1,137	1,562	1,704	1,468
1930	1,137	1,400	1,605	1,381
1931	1,008	1,250	1,436	1,231
1932	923	1,125	1,284	1,111
1933	876	1,125	1,316	1,106
1934	791	1,175	1,359	1,108
1935	780	1,225	1,714	1,240
1936	836	1,262	1,800	1,299
1937	836	1,321	1,901	1,353
1938	836	1,321	1,882	1,346
1939	836	1,321	1,889	1,349
1940	836	1,321	1,896	1,351
1941	836	1,343	1,919	1,366
1942	993	1,647	2,529	1,723
1943	1,215	1,662	2,658	1,845
1944	1,379	1,675	2,719	1,924
1945	1,498	2,070	2,810	2,124
1946	1,627	2,500	3,050	2,392
1947	1,929	2,675	3,325	2,643
1948	2,107	2,858	3,635	2,867
1949	1,990	2,925	3,715	2,877
1950	1,932	3,000	3,800	2,911
1951	2,171	3,195	4,020	3,129
1952	2,171	3,200	4,250	3,207
1953	2,444	3,279	4,500	3,408
1954	2,444	3,500	4,766	3,570
1955	2,444	3,839	4,900	3,728
1956	2,444	3,920	5,200	3,855
1957	2,444	4,050	5,200	3,898
1958	2,662	4,230	5,200	4,031
1959	2,662	4,250	5,200	4,037
1960	2,662	4,348	5,609	4,206

TABLE   B   The Poverty Band, 1905-60, in Constant 1960 Dollars

Year	"Minimum Subsistence"	"Minimum Adequacy"	"Minimum Comfort"	Mid-point of Band	Index: Men's Low Wages
1905	1,386	2,098	2,437	1,974	1,474
1906	1,355	2,051	2,383	1,920	1,549
1907	1,297	1,963	2,280	1,847	1,514
1908	1,325	2,006	2,408	1,913	1,380
1909	1,419	2,083	2,550	2,017	1,474
1910	1,434	2,054	2,544	2,011	1,480
1911	1,520	2,126	2,638	2,095	1,493
1912	1,571	2,146	2,683	2,133	1,507
1913	1,637	2,158	2,727	2,174	1,527
1914	1,717	2,213	2,780	2,237	1,481
1915	1,809	2,261	3,063	2,378	1,499
1916	1,725	2,322	3,224	2,424	1,643
1917	1,515	2,195	3,055	2,255	1,651
1918	1,629	2,613	3,044	2,428	1,798
1919	1,797	2,432	3,227	2,485	1,648
1920	1,665	2,193	3,066	2,308	1,669
1921	1,666	2,337	3,075	2,359	1,553
1922	1,861	2,495	3,244	2,533	1,598
1923	1,854	2,517	3,160	2,510	1,729
1924	1,874	2,628	3,114	2,539	1,708
1925	1,844	2,635	2,994	2,491	1,672
1926	1,901	2,677	2,948	2,509	1,685
1927	1,936	2,706	2,965	2,536	1,728
1928	1,958	2,715	2,955	2,543	1,738
1929	1,960	2,693	2,938	2,530	1,721
1930	2,015	2,481	2,844	2,467	1,650
1931	1,963	2,434	2,796	2,398	1,632
1932	1,998	2,436	2,780	2,405	1,528
1933	2,003	2,572	3,008	2,528	1,605
1934	1,750	2,599	3,006	2,452	1,648
1935	1,682	2,641	3,695	2,673	1,708
1936	1,783	2,692	3,839	2,771	1,798
1937	1,722	2,721	3,916	2,786	1,747
1938	1,754	2,771	3,948	2,824	1,645
1939	1,780	2,812	4,022	2,871	1,782
1940	1,765	2,789	4,002	2,852	1,900
1941	1,682	2,702	3,861	2,738	2,161
1942	1,803	2,991	4,592	3,129	2,457
1943	2,078	2,842	4,545	3,155	2,770
1944	2,318	2,816	4,571	3,235	2,959
1945	2,463	3,403	4,620	3,495	2,833
1946	2,468	3,793	4,627	3,629	2,620
1947	2,556	3,544	4,406	3,502	2,654
1948	2,594	3,518	4,475	3,529	2,648
1949	2,474	3,636	4,618	3,576	2,699

T A B L E   B   The Poverty Band, 1905-60, in Constant 1960 Dollars (Continued)

Year	"Minimum Subsistence"	"Minimum Adequacy"	"Minimum Comfort"	Mid-point of Band	Index: Men's Low Wages
		Budget Level			
1950	2,378	3,693	4,678	3,583	2,872
1951	2,473	3,639	4,579	3,564	2,869
1952	2,418	3,565	4,735	3,573	3,000
1953	2,703	3,627	4,977	3,790	3,077
1954	2,691	3,854	5,247	3,931	3,035
1955	2,701	4,242	5,415	4,119	3,291
1956	2,659	4,265	5,658	4,194	3,373
1957	2,571	4,261	5,470	4,101	3,331
1958	2,726	4,332	5,325	4,128	3,369
1959	2,702	4,314	5,278	4,098	3,524
1960	2,662	4,348	5,609	4,206	3,468

Standards for Food and Housing for a Family of Four in Selected Budgets, 1908, 1935, and 1960 (Constant 1960 Dollars)

Content	"Subsistence" Budgets		
	1908 Fall River, BLS (1)	1935 N.Y.C., Charity (2)	1960 N.Y.C., Welfare (3)
1. Total annual budget	$1,360	$2,060	$2,660
2. Food, $ per year	$ 770	$ 810	$1,320
3. High-protein foods, lbs./wk.[a]	21.7	32.2	54.7
4. Farinaceous foods, lbs./wk.	47.4	29.7	33.9
5. Tobacco & alcoholic bev., $ per year	0	0	0
6. Ratio of high-protein (line 3) to farinaceous foods (line 4)	46%	108%	161%
7. Ratio of food (line 2) to total budget (line 1)	57%	39%	50%
8. Housing: shelter, heat & utilities, $ per year	$ 340	$ 480	$ 680
	4 rooms; no bath; inside toilet; stove heat	2-3 rooms; 1 coal stove; ice in summer; toilet for every 2 families; clean; accessible	5 rooms
9. Ratio of food & housing to total budget	82%	63%	75%
10. Electricity, kw./yr.	N.A.	ca. 200	N.A.
For:	N.A.	Lights	Lights, refrigeration, iron
11. Telephone calls	N.A.	None	None
12. Transportation	N.A.	520 carfares	520 carfares

Content	"Adequacy" Budgets		
	1908 Fall River, BLS (4)	1935 U.S. Cities WPA (5)	1960 N.Y.C., Charity (6)
1. Total annual budget	$2,060	$2,720	$4,460
2. Food, $ per year	$ 880	$ 950	$1,650
3. High-protein foods, lbs./wk.[a]	23.4	44.6	62.7
4. Farinaceous foods, lbs./wk.	46.8	32.1	30.9
5. Tobacco & alcoholic bev., $ per year	0	$ 10	$ 50
6. Ratio of high-protein (line 3) to farinaceous foods (line 4)	43%	139%	203%
7. Ratio of food (line 2) to total budget (line 1)	43%	35%	37%
8. Housing: shelter, heat & utilities, $ per year	$ 490	$ 550	$ 890
	4 rooms; bath; wood and coal heat; gas light	4 rooms; ice year round; bathroom; clean; safe	5 rooms; bathroom; safe; accessible
9. Ratio of food & housing to total budget	66%	56%	57%
10. Electricity, kw./yr. For:	N.A.	271 Lights, iron, radio	960 Lights, refrigeration, iron, toaster, vacuum cleaner, fan
11. Telephone calls	N.A.	Occasional calls, public booth	Minimum-cost subscription
12. Transportation	N.A.	780 carfares	988 fares + vacation (50-mile round trip by rail)

Content	"Comfort" Budgets		
	1908 N.Y.C., Chapin (7)	1935 San Francisco, Heller (8)	1960 N.Y.C., BLS (9)
1. Total annual budget	$2,320	$3,700	$5,400
2. Food, $ per year	$1,010	$1,100	$1,820
3. High-protein foods, lbs./wk. [a]	25.9	61.1	69.6
4. Farinaceous foods, lbs./wk.	24.0	26.0	22.2
5. Tobacco & alcoholic bev., $ per year	$ 125	$ 50	$ 145
		182 pkg. cigarettes	304 pkg. cigarettes, 51 cigars, 13 oz. pipe tobacco
6. Ratio of high-protein (line 3) to farinaceous foods (line 4)	108%	235%	314%
7. Ratio of food (line 2) to total budget (line 1)	43%	29%	33%
8. Housing: shelter, heat & utilities, $ per year	$ 690	$ 700	$1,030
	3 rooms; decent; sanitary	5 rooms; elec. refrigeration; bathroom	5 rooms; 70°; bathroom; play space; 10 blocks to transportation
9. Ratio of food & housing to total budget	69%	49%	53%
10. Electricity, kw./yr.	N.A.	732 + natural gas	1,500
For:	N.A.	Lights, refrigeration, iron, radio, vacuum cleaner, washing machine	Lights, refrigeration, iron, toaster, vacuum cleaner, washing machine, food mixer, sewing machine
11. Telephone calls	N.A.	2-party subscription, 60 calls per month	Minimum-cost subscription, 65 message units per month

Content	"Comfort" Budgets		
	1908 N.Y.C., Chapin (7)	1935 San Fran- cisco,Heller (8)	1960 N.Y.C., BLS (9)
12. Transportation	N.A.	Auto 2 yrs. old, replaced every 4 years, plus 900 pub- lic carfares	Used auto about 4 yrs. old, every 3 yrs. for 48% of families, plus 329 pub- lic fares, plus 124 miles (rail) out of city. For non- auto owners, 710 public fares & 244 miles out of city.

Sources: Cols. 1 and 4: "Family Budgets of Typical Cotton Mill Workers in Fall River, Mass.," University of Chicago Press, 1914. Cols. 2 and 3: New York City Department of Welfare, unpublished material. Col. 5: Margaret L. Stecker, Inter-City Differences in Costs of Living in March 1935, 59 Cities, Works Progress Administration, Monograph XII, Washington, 1937; and Quantity Budgets for Basic Maintenance and Emergency Standards of Living, Works Progress Administration, Division of Social Research, Series 1, No. 21, Washington, 1936. Col. 6: Annual Price Survey and Family Budget Cost, Community Council of Greater New York, New York, 1961. Col. 7: Robert C. Chapin, The Standard of Living Among Work-ingmen's Families in New York City, Russell Sage Foundation, New York Charities Publication Committee, 1909. Col. 8: Quantity and Cost Budgets, Heller Commit-tee for Research in Social Economics, University of California, Berkeley, 1935. Col. 9: U.S. Bureau of Labor Statistics, "The Interim City Worker's Family Bud-get," Monthly Labor Review, Reprint No. 2346, 1960.

a. Quarts of milk and milk products are added to pounds of other foods.

Note: The budgets for 1908 were originally for five persons; they were converted to four by dividing by 114. The same factor was used for converting the housing cost. The method provides only the roughest approximation, especially for housing as a third child would probably not require an extra room. Total dollar values of these specific budgets do not necessarily correspond to the values for corresponding levels of need shown in Table B of Appendix 2.

APPENDIX 4   Distribution of Family Personal Income, 1935–59 (Families and Unattached Individuals)

	Per Cent of Income								Per Cent Changes		
	1935/36	1941	1947	1950	1953	1955	1958	1959	1935/36-53	1953-59	1935/36-59
Total	100.0	100.0	100.0	100.0	100.0	100.0	100.0	100.0	–	–	–
Lowest fifth	4.1	4.1	5.0	4.8	4.9	4.8	4.6	4.5	+19	-8	+ 9.7
Second fifth	9.2	9.5	11.0	10.9	11.3	11.3	10.9	10.9	+23	-3.5	+18
Third fifth	14.1	15.3	16.0	16.1	16.6	16.4	16.2	16.2	+18	-2.4	+14.9
Fourth fifth	20.9	22.3	22.0	22.1	22.5	22.3	22.7	22.7	+ 7.6	+2.2	+ 8.6
Highest fifth	51.7	48.8	46.0	46.1	44.7	45.2	45.6	45.7	-13.5	+2.2	-11.6
Top 5 per cent	26.5	24.0	20.9	21.4	19.9	20.3	19.9	19.9	-25	no change	-25

Source: Statistical Abstract of the United States, 1961.

Calculation of the Number of Poor

Utilizing the three levels of need set forth in Appendix 2, the New School poverty study staff calculated the number of persons in the United States who failed to meet these income levels in the period 1929 to 1960. This count, presented in Table A following, was made by the following method.

The distribution of family personal income, as reported by the Office of Business Economics, U.S. Department of Commerce, was the basic measure used. This measure of income after taxes provides a better indication of "command over goods and services" than does money income alone, since personal income includes such items as imputed rent of owner-occupied homes, the value of food and fuel produced and consumed on farms, and the value of perquisites received by civilian workers. Some types of free goods, and borrowing power, are not accounted for in the personal income series and yet represent command over goods and services. Their magnitude cannot be estimated accurately. In a sense, however, the levels of need, derived from budgets, make allowance for some of these items. For example, certain budgets recognize the use of free recreation facilities; at the lowest budget levels, some free medical care is generally assumed. Our calculations do not allow for the possibility that higher income families take more advantage of free goods and services than lower income families do. It is felt, however, that this does not seriously impair the procedure. The fact that families with higher income have greater access to credit may be slightly more important, at the "minimum comfort" budget level at least; but recent budgets at this level have included the costs associated with installment purchases. No adjustments were made in our calculations for temporary poverty, or for temporarily high income.

Distributions of family personal income are available separately for families and for unattached individuals in the civilian population. For the years 1941 through 1960 our basic data were obtained from the annual estimates of family personal income by the Office of Business Economics as reported in the Survey of Current Business (issue of March 1958 for the years 1941-53, May issue for each of the subsequent years). The income distributions for the other years, 1929 and 1935-36, are necessarily rough, but they appeared to be adequate for our purposes. Our income distributions for 1929 were taken from America's Capacity to Consume, by Maurice Leven, Harold G. Moulton, and Clark Warburton (The Brookings Institution, Washington, 1934). The 1935-36 distributions are based on the estimate developed by Selma Goldsmith et al. in the Review of Economics and Statistics, February 1954, which is conceptually similar to, but not part of, the official series of the Office of Business Economics.

The budget standards from which we started were for four-person families. We adjusted them for variations in family size only to the extent of estimating an "average need" based on changes from year to year in average family size. The average need of a three-person family was estimated at 87.0 per cent of that of a four-person family, on the basis of data developed by the Bureau of Labor Statistics and presented in the Monthly Labor Review, November 1960. Straight-line interpolation was used to estimate family needs when the average size of families was between three and four persons. The needs of unattached individuals were taken to be one-half of these adjusted family needs.

Taking into account the number of persons per average family in different years, we then combined the figures for families and unattached individuals to obtain the total number of persons whose income was below each level. In 1960, for example, when there were 45,370,000 families and 10,690,000 unattached individuals and the average family size was 3.7 persons, the procedure was as follows:

	"Subsistence"	"Adequacy"	"Comfort"
1. Budget standard for a 4-person family in 1960	$ 2,660	$ 4,350	$ 5,610
Families:			
2. Income needed per family of 1960 average size to meet this standard (96% of line 1)	$ 2,554	$ 4,176	$ 5,386
3. Per cent of families below this income level	10.7	25.0	39.0
4. Number of families, in thousands (line 3 x 45,370)	4,855	11,342	17,694
5. Number of persons in these families, in thousands (line 4 x 3.7 persons per family)	17,964	41,965	65,468
Unattached Individuals:			
6. Income needed by each (48% of line 1)	$ 1,277	$ 2,088	$ 2,693
7. Per cent of unattached individuals below this income level	18.0	38.5	50.0
8. Number of such individuals, in thousands (line 7 x 10,690)	1,924	4,116	5,345
Total:			
9. Total number of persons with income below adjusted budget standard, in thousands (line 5 plus line 8)	19,888	46,081	70,813

Some of these data differ from those presented elsewhere because different sources were used.

The percentages of households below each budget level, also included in Table A, were computed on the basis of total households (consumer units) as estimated by the Office of Business Economics.

All of these calculations were in terms of contemporary standards in the then current dollars. The number of poor so measured is compared in Table B with the number obtained when 1960 budget standards, expressed in constant dollars, are extended backward to earlier years. For this purpose the 1960 standards were deflated by the Personal Consumption Expenditure Index of the Office of Business Economics.

TABLE   A   Number and Per Cent Below Three Budget Levels, by Contemporary Standards, 1929-60

Year	Below "Minimum Subsistence" Level		Below "Minimum Adequacy" Level		Below "Minimum Comfort" Level	
	Number of Persons (Millions)	Per Cent of Households	Number of Persons (Millions)	Per Cent of Households	Number of Persons (Millions)	Per Cent of Households
1929	31.8	26	52.2	43	57.8	48
1935-36	33.9	27	57.3	46	80.3	64
1941	21.6	17	41.5	32	62.9	48
1944	12.1	10	19.2	15	56.1	45
1947	21.3	15	38.1	27	55.4	39
1950	20.1	14	41.8	28	61.0	41
1951	18.9	12	37.4	25	55.4	37
1952	17.8	12	33.2	22	56.1	36
1953	22.7	14	35.7	23	61.1	39
1954	23.0	14	42.7	27	69.7	44
1955	19.9	12	45.3	28	69.6	43
1956	18.1	11	42.4	26	72.5	44
1957	17.7	10	42.9	25	67.3	40
1958	22.7	13	49.0	28	70.5	41
1959	21.3	12	46.8	27	65.2	37
1960	19.9	11	46.1	26	70.8	40

Note: The marked discontinuity in numbers and percentages between 1941 and 1944 and between 1944 and 1947 is due to the combination of the following factors: the table deals with civilian population only; there was a significant change in income distribution during these years; and there was a large upgrading of budget standards between 1944 and 1947 while between 1941 and 1944 budget standards remained relatively unchanged.

T A B L E   B   Number of Persons Below Three Budget Levels in Selected
Years, by Contemporary Standards and by 1960 Standards
(Millions of Persons)

Year and Budget Level	Contemporary Standards in Current Dollars	1960 Standards in Constant Dollars	Difference
1929			
"Comfort"	57.8	94.9	37.1
"Adequacy"	52.2	81.9	29.7
"Subsistence"	31.8	48.7	16.9
1935-36			
"Comfort"	80.3	101.7	21.4
"Adequacy"	57.3	87.8	30.5
"Subsistence"	33.9	49.9	16.0
1941			
"Comfort"	62.9	87.8	24.9
"Adequacy"	41.5	68.2	26.7
"Subsistence"	21.6	39.1	17.5
1947			
"Comfort"	55.4	80.8	25.4
"Adequacy"	38.1	55.7	17.6
"Subsistence"	21.3	23.5	2.2
1950			
"Comfort"	61.0	79.4	18.4
"Adequacy"	41.8	54.4	12.6
"Subsistence"	20.1	24.5	4.4
1955			
"Comfort"	69.6	74.6	5.0
"Adequacy"	45.3	47.9	2.6
"Subsistence"	19.9	19.7	-0.2
1960			
"Comfort"	70.8	70.8	--
"Adequacy"	46.1	46.1	--
"Subsistence"	19.9	19.9	--

APPENDIX 6   Per Cent Having Specified Characteristics, in Total Population and by Income Class, 1960

Characteristic	All Families	I. Families with Income of:									
		$0-$500	$500-$1,000	$1,000-$1,500	$1,500-$2,000	$2,000-$2,500	$2,500-$3,000	$3,000-$3,500	$3,500-$4,000	$4,000-$4,500	$4,500-$5,000
All families:											
Number (thousands)	45,435	1,136	1,136	1,727	1,908	2,145	1,908	2,226	2,226	2,363	2,408
Per cent	100.0	2.5	2.5	3.8	4.2	4.7	4.2	4.9	4.9	5.2	5.3
Non-white	9.5	21.7	29.3	25.6	18.4	17.2	15.2	14.6	12.7	9.7	9.2
Female head	10.1	32.5	32.5	24.3	21.5	19.6	18.9	14.9	12.4	8.4	8.8
Head age 65 or over	13.6	17.4	32.7	37.0	38.7	35.2	28.6	19.0	14.5	11.0	10.8
Head age 14 to 24	5.1	6.5	8.6	6.3	7.5	7.8	7.9	8.7	10.1	8.2	6.2
Rural farm	7.7	28.6	25.8	19.0	15.9	13.8	14.8	11.1	9.9	7.2	5.9
No earners	7.3	35.2	31.4	29.6	33.5	28.0	14.4	6.7	4.9	2.9	1.8
Six or more children under 18	2.5	6.2	2.9	3.8	4.2	3.8	4.8	3.4	3.3	2.1	2.4
Cumulative:											
Per cent	55.8	148.1	163.2	145.6	139.7	125.4	104.6	78.4	67.8	49.5	45.1
Index[a]	100.0	265.4	292.4	260.9	250.3	224.7	187.4	140.5	121.5	88.7	80.8

Characteristic	All Unattached Individuals	II. Unattached Individuals with Income of:							
		$0-$500	$500-$1,000	$1,000-$1,500	$1,500-$2,000	$2,000-$2,500	$2,500-$3,000	$3,000-$3,500	$3,500-$4,000
All unattached individuals:									
Number (thousands)	10,900	1,591	2,071	1,450	785	796	600	578	534
Per cent	100.0	14.6	19.0	13.3	7.2	7.3	5.5	5.3	4.9
Non-white	13.7	18.5	20.8	12.9	10.8	15.1	14.7	10.4	7.3
Female	61.5	72.0	73.1	63.8	65.1	62.3	61.5	63.8	62.7
Age 65 or over	33.5	31.4	60.0	53.7	48.4	28.4	19.5	15.2	15.7
Age 14 to 24	10.0	17.7	6.8	6.3	10.3	10.4	10.8	19.0	13.1
Rural farm	3.4	7.5	4.3	9.5	2.8	1.6	1.2	1.2	2.2
Non-earner	37.0	70.3	63.9	57.1	39.6	17.2	14.8	9.0	12.2
Cumulative:									
Per cent	159.1	217.4	228.9	203.3	177.0	135.0	122.5	118.6	110.2
Index[a]	100.0	136.6	143.9	127.8	111.3	84.9	77.0	74.5	69.3

Source: Current Population Reports, Bureau of the Census, 1960, Series P60-37.

a. Cumulative per cent converted to index. Total = 100.0

Note: Discrepancies between figures shown in this table and in other tables are due to the different sources used.

Per Cent of Those with Specified Characteristics Having Low Income, 1960

Characteristic (of family head where applicable)	Income Class				
	$0-$500		$0-$2,000		$0-$4,500
	Families	Unattached Individuals	Families	Unattached Individuals	Families
Total population	2.5	14.6	13.0	54.1[a]	36.7
Non-white	5.7	19.7	31.7	66.7	65.8
Female	8.0	17.1	34.0	60.9	68.0
Age:					
65 or over	3.2	13.7	31.4	79.4	68.0
14 to 24	3.2	25.9	18.3	54.9	58.0
Residence:					
Rural farm	9.3	32.0	35.8	79.9	70.3
Southern					
All	N.A.	N.A.	21.3	66.3	50.3
Non-white	N.A.	N.A.	44.0	78.7	80.8
Non-earner	12.1	27.7	57.9	88.7	93.4
Work experience:					
None	7.2	21.0	40.3	86.3	76.8
Part time	6.2	20.6	39.6	80.4	71.0
0-26 weeks	8.0	26.3	49.3	86.5	81.9
27-49 weeks	4.2	12.0	32.3	82.4	64.0
Six or more children under 18	6.2	--	22.0	--	54.2
Less than 8 years of schooling[b]	6.2	22.6	33.2	80.3	69.7

Sources: Current Population Reports, Bureau of the Census, 1960, Series P60-37. Education data from Current Population Reports, 1956, Series P60-27. Southern residence material from special tabulation by the Census Bureau (unpublished data).

a. This figure does not match that shown in Appendix 14 because a different source was used.

b. 1956 used because data were not available for 1960; see source. The percentages of the U.S. population in these income categories in 1956 were: for families, $0-$500, 3.2; $0-$2,000, 15.4; $0-$4,500, 46.1; for unattached individuals, $0-$500, 17.7; $0-2,000, 61.1.

Measurement of Degree of Attachment Between Characteristics and Income Level

The Pi coefficient was used by the New School poverty study staff to compare the income status of two populations, one with and one without a given characteristic (e. g., non-white vs. white). Income status was defined as income above or below a given level. The Pi coefficient (r) was obtained by the following formula:

$$r = \text{cosine} \left[3.1416 \; \frac{\sqrt{bc}}{\sqrt{ad} + \sqrt{bc}} \right]$$

The components of the formula were:

	number below income level	number above income level
number with given characteristic	a	b
number without given characteristic	c	d

Multiplying a x d yields a measure of the strength of the association between possession of the characteristic and the particular income level; multiplying b x c, a measure of the weakness of the association. The formula gives a value which represents the net effect of these sets of data. The mechanical processes of finding square roots, multiplying by Pi, and using a cosine table are simply the means whereby the relationship is expressed in a manageable form: all values will fall between +1 and -1.

The degree of attachment so obtained, for seven characteristics at three levels of low income, is shown in Tables A, B, and C. For 1960, $2,500, $4,500 and $5,500 were selected as the appropriate low-level incomes. For earlier years these levels were corrected for changes in the Consumer Price Index and rounded out to the nearest $250. The equivalent levels for individuals and the calculation of the numbers of families and individuals falling below them were computed in the manner used in obtaining the number of the poor falling below the poverty band described in Appendix 2.

TABLE A   Degree of Attachment (Pi Coefficients) Between Specified
Characteristics and "Very Low" Income Levels, 1947-60

I. Families

Year	No Earners	Non-white	Head 65 or Over	Rural Farm	Female Head	6 or More Children Under 18	Head 14 to 24 Years of Age
1947	.7547	.5052	.5712	.4975	.3611	N.A.	.1392
1948	.7660	.4772	.5225	.5100	.3420	.2476	.0175
1949	.7660	N.A.	.4746	.6018	.3934	.2700	.1161
1950	.7698	N.A.	.5398	.5050	.5100	.2560	.1650
1951	.8587	N.A.	.6225	.5324	.5100	.2419	.0987
1952	.8274	N.A.	.5688	.5519	.5100	.2306	.2391
1954	.7986	.4514	.5200	.5854	.4772	.1994	.2051
1955	.7808	.4797	.5446	.6018	.5150	.2164	.2363
1956	.7844	.4874	.5446	.6041	.5025	.1421	.1334
1957	.7753	.5050	.5446	.5901	.5125	.1965	.1103
1958	.7698	.5250	.5100	.5495	.5544	.2952	.1363
1959	.7451	.5446	.4975	.5422	.5544	.2504	.2447
1960	.7071	.4975	.4410	.5495	.5348	.2391	.2447

II. Unattached Individuals

Year	Non-earner	Non-white	Age 65 or Over	Rural Farm	Female	Age 14 to 24
1947	.4384	.1392	.3173	.2108	.2784	.1937
1948	.6734	.1536	.2532	.4772	.2193	.3448
1949	.6472	.N.A.	.4067	.3961	.2700	.4848
1950	.6157	N.A.	.3557	.3881	.2560	.4041
1951	.7880	N.A.	.6202	.2840	.2616	.1679
1952	.7790	N.A.	.5568	.4436	.3448	.2476
1954	.7214	.2193	.4720	.2979	.2532	.2164
1955	.7071	.2022	.4566	.3934	.2504	.1650
1956	.6967	.1536	.4305	.3365	.2250	.2812
1957	.7214	.2278	.4617	.2560	.2221	.2756
1958	.7112	.2079	.4436	.3448	.2447	.2672
1959	.6841	.2363	.3773	.4794	.2221	.2419
1960	.6539	.2784	.3907	.3638	.2840	.2616

TABLE   B   Degree of Attachment (Pi Coefficients) Between Specified
             Characteristics and "Middle Low" Income Levels, 1947-60

I. Families

Year	No Earners	Non-white	Head 65 or Over	Rural Farm	Female Head	6 or More Children Under 18	Head 14 to 24 Years of Age
1947	.7698	.5736	.4797	.4669	.3529	N.A.	.2560
1948	.8403	.5324	.5100	.4899	.3420	.2644	.1994
1949	.8496	N.A.	.4874	.5948	.3800	.3256	.2700
1950	.8274	N.A.	.5125	.5000	.4874	.2979	.2672
1951	.8843	N.A.	.5664	.5398	.4823	.2644	.1908
1952	.8557	N.A.	.5348	.5348	.5050	.2419	.2868
1954	.8465	.4669	.5324	.5901	.5000	.2051	.2644
1955	.8418	.4772	.5783	.6111	.5050	.2476	.2644
1956	.8511	.5075	.5736	.5925	.5025	.1851	.1965
1957	.8480	.5000	.5972	.5712	.5175	.1994	.2221
1958	.8660	.5299	.5878	.5299	.5398	.2896	.3145
1959	.8403	.5225	.5807	.5422	.5495	.2476	.2868
1960	.8418	.4772	.5736	.5250	.5250	.2560	.3173

II. Unattached Individuals

Year	Non-earner	Non-white	Age 65 or Over	Rural Farm	Female	Age 14 to 24
1947	.5807	.1965	.4950	.3145	.2476	.1421
1948	.7623	.1937	.5250	.4410	.2108	.3062
1949	.8241	N.A.	.6157	.3746	.2672	.4592
1950	.7771	N.A.	.6018	.3502	.2924	.2756
1951	.7916	N.A.	.6225	.3145	.2672	.1622
1952	.7716	N.A.	.5592	.4410	.3256	.2419
1954	.7274	.2051	.4924	.3529	.2447	.2221
1955	.7173	.2051	.4848	.4041	.2504	.1736
1956	.7173	.1363	.4617	.3311	.2391	.2672
1957	.7294	.2447	.4874	.2419	.2306	.2784
1958	.7333	.2079	.4950	.3448	.2419	.2728
1959	.7092	.2164	.4384	.4794	.2278	.2334
1960	.6926	.2644	.4514	.3934	.2700	.2391

TABLE   C   Degree of Attachment (Pi Coefficients) Between Specified
             Characteristics and "High Low" Income Levels, 1947-60

I. Families

Year	No Earners	Non-white	Head 65 or Over	Rural Farm	Female Head	6 or More Children Under 18	Head 14 to 24 Years of Age
1947	..7112	.5398	.2979	.3420	.2504	N.A.	.4924
1948	.8107	.5483	.3475	.4173	.3145	.2868	.3311
1949	.8192	N.A.	.3584	.5495	.2952	.3118	.3611
1950	.7898	N.A.	.4014	.4669	.4462	.2391	.3145
1951	.8258	N.A.	.4173	.4669	.3746	.2728	.3256
1952	.8496	N.A.	.4173	.4643	.4848	.3118	.4147
1954	.8192	.5348	.4514	.5422	.4410	.2812	.4305
1955	.8511	.5275	.4924	.5854	.4720	.2560	.4067
1956	.8557	.5471	.5175	.5712	.4695	.2532	.3448
1957	.8572	.5150	.5519	.5592	.4823	.2868	.3746
1958	.8910	.5471	.5471	.5125	.5025	.3173	.4226
1959	.8746	.5348	.5422	.5519	.5324	.2672	.4462
1960	.8829	.4848	.5616	.5422	.5200	.2840	.4305

II. Unattached Individuals

Year	Non-earner	Non-white	Age 65 or Over	Rural Farm	Female	Age 14 to 24
1947	.5495	.4384	.5299	.4067	.3228	.3338
1948	:7808	.3201	.5831	.4695	.2334	.3961
1949	.8290	N.A.	.5831	.5000	.2784	.4592
1950	.7844	N.A.	.6225	.3448	.2924	.2504
1951	.8450	N.A.	.6691	.4695	.3692	.2672
1952	.8021	N.A.	.5878	.4305	.3365	.3393
1954	.7735	.2840	.3283	.5150	.3035	.2136
1955	.8021	.3201	.6406	.5664	.2784	.2136
1956	.8434	.2136	.6338	.6134	.2868	.2560
1957	.8192	.2560	.6134	.4924	.2840	.2924
1958	.8387	.2672	.6450	.4173	.2616	.2952
1959	.8021	.2812	.6018	.4899	.2588	.2250
1960	.8021	.2700	.6406	.4279	.2868	.2419

The Convergence of
Poverty-Linked Characteristics

In considering how the relationship of one or more family characteristics to poverty might be gauged, the New School poverty study
staff posited a heuristic model. The model assigned a continuum of
numerical values, indicating the theoretical degree to which each factor would induce poverty.. For the model, the staff selected subnormal education and poor health as the two interacting characteristics.

Let us assume that the likelihood that an individual will have less
than nine years of schooling is five out of ten; less than six years,
four out of ten; and no schooling at all, one out of ten. Similarly, let
us posit the chance of various degrees of disability to be five, three,
and two out of ten for slight, moderate, and extreme disability. The
hypothetical joint frequency distribution resulting from the interaction
of these two traits can be represented by values of 25 for less than
nine years of schooling and slight disability, 15 for less than nine
years of schooling and moderate disability, and so on. These values
are plotted below:

Degree of Disability

	Slight (5)	Moderate (3)	Extreme (2)
Less than nine (5)	A 25	D 15	G 10
Less than six (4)	B 20	E 12	H 8
None (1)	C 5	F 3	I 2

(Rows labeled under "Years of Schooling")

Box I—no schooling and extreme disability—would contain the
smallest percentage of the total population, but that part with the
greatest risk of being poor. Conversely, Box A would include a relatively large share of the population, but their slight educational deficiencies and slight disability would imply a lesser risk of being poor.

The model could be extended to take account of several characteristics, and also for changes over time.

In this hypothetical example it is assumed that the traits are not interlinked. Presence of low education is not in itself assumed to make for a greater than normal chance of an individual also being disabled, or vice versa. Restructuring the example to show that, on the contrary, the very poorly educated are more apt to be seriously disabled (which is likely to be the case) would yield a different set of values. In this case, box I (lower right corner) and boxes E, F, and H (surrounding it) would have higher frequencies.

The detailed analysis of the congruence of poverty-linked characteristics carried out in the New School study was limited to a single year, 1960, and to those few characteristics for which data were available. The results are presented in Appendices 10 and 11.

Families Having One to Four Specified Characteristics as Per Cent of All Families at the Same Income Level, 1960

Characteristic(s) of Family Head	Total Families in U.S.		Below "Subsistence" ($2,660)		Below "Adequacy" ($4,350)		Below "Comfort" ($5,610)	
	Number	Per Cent	Number	Per Cent	Number	Per Cent	Number	Per Cent
Total families in U.S.	45,128,397	100.0	8,370,561	100.0	15,668,321	100.0	22,284,463	100.0
One Characteristic								
Total	11,883,711	26.3	4,235,237	50.6	6,939,046	44.3	8,467,687	38.0
Aged (65 or over)	4,276,016	100.0		39.6		60.2		70.5
Female	2,387,443	100.0		38.0		60.4		73.3
Rural farm	2,434,041	100.0		34.5		57.5		71.0
Non-white	2,786,211	100.0		28.6		54.7		70.9
Two Characteristics								
Total	2,634,027	5.8	1,452,879	17.4	1,927,803	12.3	2,152,289	9.7
Aged, female	787,975	100.0		37.2		56.1		68.4
Aged, rural farm	489,732	100.0		54.9		74.7		83.2
Aged, non-white	331,316	100.0		62.6		80.1		87.5
Female, rural farm	73,842	100.0		54.8		73.9		83.1
Female, non-white	743,115	100.0		64.6		82.2		88.4
Rural farm, non-white	208,047	100.0		78.3		90.8		94.8
Three Characteristics								
Total	234,573	.5	159,888	1.9	194,878	1.2	209,375	.9
Aged, female, rural farm	55,444	100.0		52.5		70.8		80.3
Aged, female, non-white	115,444	100.0		67.5		83.5		89.8
Aged, rural farm, non-white	40,901	100.0		81.1		91.9		95.4
Female, rural farm, non-white	22,784	100.0		86.6		94.9		97.8
Four Characteristics								
Total	7,698	.02	6,469	.08	7,227	.05	7,469	.03
Aged, female, rural farm, non-white	7,698	100.0		84.0		93.9		97.0
All characteristics and combinations	14,760,009	32.7	5,854,471	69.9	9,068,954	57.9	10,836,820	48.6

Source: U.S. Census of Population, 1960, United States Summary, Detailed Characteristics PC(1) 1D. There is no double counting; those with two characteristics, for example, form a separate and additional increment.

Families Having One to Four Specified Characteristics as Per Cent of All Families with Such Characteristics, by Income Level, 1960

Characteristic(s) of Family Head	Income Level		
	Below "Subsistence" ($2,660)	Below "Adequacy" ($4,350)	Below "Comfort" ($5,610)
Total number of families with one or more specified characteristics	5,854,471	9,068,954	10,836,820
	100.0	100.0	100.0
1. Aged (65 or over)	28.9	28.3	27.8
2. Female	15.5	15.9	16.2
3. Rural farm	14.3	15.4	15.9
4. Non-white	13.6	16.8	18.2
5. Non-white, female	8.2	6.7	6.1
6. Aged, female	5.0	4.9	5.0
7. Aged, rural farm	4.6	4.0	3.8
8. Non-white, aged	3.5	2.9	2.7
9. Non-white, rural farm	2.8	2.1	1.8
10. Aged, non-white, female	1.3	1.1	1.0
11. Rural farm, female	.7	.6	.6
12. Non-white, rural farm, aged	.6	.4	.4
13. Rural farm, aged, female	.5	.4	.4
14. Rural farm, non-white, female	.3	.2	.2
15. Non-white, rural farm, aged, female	.1	.08	.07

Source: Same as Appendix 10.

Note: In the category below the "subsistence" budget level, the combined percentages, by characteristic, when each characteristic is taken alone or in combination with any other, are: aged, 44.5; female, 31.6; non-white, 30.4; rural farm, 23.9.

APPENDIX 12

Per Cent at Low Income Levels,
by Size of Urban Place, 1960

Income	Size of Place[a]				
	1,000,000 or Over	250,000- 1,000,000	50,000- 250,000	25,000- 50,000	2,500-25,000
	I. Families				
Below $2,500	10.3	14.0	15.3	17.1	18.6
Below $3,500	16.6	22.5	25.7	28.7	28.8
Below $4,500	25.9	32.2	35.7	39.5	39.7
Median income	$6,486	$5,941	$5,566	$5,343	$5,356
	II. Unattached Individuals				
Below $1,000	23.4	29.0	33.7	26.4	37.4
Below $2,000	42.4	52.2	54.7	46.8	61.6
Below $3,000	55.1	67.1	67.1	65.5	74.3
Median income	$2,548	$1,876	$1,691	$2,188	$1,404

Source: Current Population Reports, Bureau of the Census, 1960, Series P60-37, Table 1, p. 25.

a. The size classes include the entire population called urban; they were prepared by combining urban areas and urban places not in urban areas as defined in the Census Annual Survey. The first three classes represent urban areas, i.e., all persons living in cities of 50,000 inhabitants or more in 1940 or according to a special census taken between 1940 and 1950. The other two classes represent the densely settled urban fringe, including both incorporated and unincorporated centers with more than 2,500 persons, surrounding these cities.

APPENDIX 13   Income Advantage of Urban over Rural Residence, 1949 and 1958

Income Level[a]	1949 Number (thousands)	Per Cent	Index of Relative Urban Advantage[b]	Income Level[a]	1958 Number (thousands)	Per Cent	Index of Relative Urban Advantage[b]	Change in Index 1949–58[c]
				I. Families				
Urban, total	25,487	100.0		Urban, total	27,192	100.0		
Below $1,000	1,708	6.7	100	Below $1,500	1,822	6.7	100	
Below $2,000	4,639	18.2	100	Below $2,500	4,106	15.1	100	
Below $3,500	12,871	50.5	100	Below $4,500	9,979	36.7	100	
Rural farm,[d] total	5,770	100.0		Rural farm,[d] total	5,004	100.0		
Below $1,000	1,973	34.2	510	Below $1,500	1,356	27.1	404	20.8
Below $2,000	3,474	60.2	331	Below $2,500	2,292	45.8	303	8.5
Below $3,500	4,899	84.9	168	Below $4,500	3,613	72.2	197	-17.3
Rural non-farm, total	7,936	100.0		Rural non-farm, total	12,006	100.0		
Below $1,500	1,032	13.0	194	Below $1,500	1,021	8.5	127	34.5
Below $2,500	2,436	30.7	169	Below $2,500	2,173	18.1	120	29.0
Below $3,500	5,309	66.9	132	Below $4,500	5,055	42.1	115	12.9
				II. Unattached Individuals				
Urban, total	6,802	100.0		Urban, total	8,338	100.0		
Below $ 500	1,449	21.3	100	Below $1,000	2,727	32.7	100	
Below $1,250	2,966	43.6	100	Below $1,250	3,294	39.5	100	
Below $2,000	4,476	65.8	100	Below $2,500	5,136	61.6	100	
Rural farm,[d] total	570	100.0		Rural farm,[d] total	616	100.0		
Below $ 500	285	50.0	235	Below $1,000	356	57.8	177	24.7
Below $1,000	404	70.8	162	Below $1,250	397	64.4	163	- 0.6
Below $2,000	512	89.8	136	Below $2,500	520	84.4	137	- 0.7

	1949				1958			
Income Level[a]	Number (thousands)	Per Cent	Index of Relative Urban Advantage[b]	Income Level[a]	Number (thousands)	Per Cent	Index of Relative Urban Advantage[b]	Change in Index 1949–58[c]
Rural non-farm, total	1,463	100.0		Rural non-farm, total	1,797	100.0		
Below $ 500	692	47.3	222	Below $1,000	846	47.1	144	35.1
Below $1,000	961	65.7	151	Below $1,250	958	53.3	135	10.6
Below $2,000	1,219	83.3	127	Below $2,500	1,312	73.0	119	6.3

Sources: Data for 1949 from Current Population Reports, Bureau of the Census, Series P60–7, Table 1, p. 20; 1958 data from Current Population Reports, Series P60–30, Table 1, p. 19.

a. The income levels selected correspond to those used in calculating the Pi coefficients for poverty-linked characteristics. Price changes are roughly accounted for by using different income levels in the two years. The Consumer Price Index rose approximately 25 per cent between 1949 and 1958 and the income levels chosen differ by approximately the same amount; for example, $3,500 for families in 1949 is compared to $4,500 in 1958. Because data were available only in $500 increments, interpolation was required in one case—the middle income level ($1,250) for unattached individuals in 1958.

b. To establish this index, the proportion of urban families and unattached individuals below each income level was set at 100, and the proportion of the rural non-farm units below the same income level was expressed as a percentage of this base.

c. The difference in urban advantage between 1949 and 1958 is here expressed as a percentage of the 1949 advantage. For example, at family income below $1,000 (and its adjusted equivalent) the advantage of urban over rural farm residence was 510 in 1949 and 404 in 1958, a difference of 106, which equals 20.8 per cent of the 1949 urban advantage. The relative advantage of urban residence has narrowed by this amount.

d. The definition of rural farm formulated in 1949 remained unchanged until 1958. This provides the longest time period covered by a consistent definition.

Per Cent of Southern Residents at Low Income Levels, 1960

	All	Urban	White	White Urban
	I. Families			
Below $2,000:				
U.S.	13.1	9.4	11.0	7.7
South	21.3	14.4	16.7	10.4
"Core-South"	27.4	17.0	20.8	10.8
Per cent difference:				
U.S. - South	63.0	53.0	52.0	35.0
U.S. - "Core-South"	109.0	81.0	89.0	40.0
Below $3,000:				
U.S.	21.4	16.4	18.6	13.8
South	33.0	24.6	27.0	18.5
"Core-South"	40.5	28.7	32.5	19.7
Per cent difference:				
U.S. - South	54.0	50.0	45.0	34.0
U.S. - "Core-South"	89.0	75.0	75.0	43.0
Below $4,000:				
U.S.	30.9	24.9	27.7	21.6
South	44.7	35.7	38.3	28.5
"Core-South"	52.7	40.6	45.0	30.8
Per cent difference:				
U.S. - South	45.0	43.0	38.0	32.0
U.S. - "Core-South"	71.0	63.0	62.0	43.0
	II. Unattached Individuals			
Below $1,000:				
U.S.	37.6	35.2	36.3	34.0
South	45.6	42.3	41.9	38.8
"Core-South"	53.6	59.6	48.7	45.6
Per cent difference:				
U.S. - South	21.0	20.0	15.0	14.0
U.S. - "Core-South"	43.0	44.0	34.0	34.0

(Continued from preceding page)

	All	Urban	White	White Urban
II. Unattached Individuals (continued)				
Below $2,000:				
U.S.	58.5	55.1	57.2	53.8
South	66.3	62.0	62.7	57.9
"Core-South"	73.0	69.1	68.9	63.1
Per cent difference:				
U.S. - South	13.0	13.0	10.0	8.0
U.S. - "Core-South"	25.0	25.0	20.0	17.0
Below $3,000:				
U.S.	70.5	67.4	68.9	65.7
South	77.5	73.9	74.1	69.8
"Core-South"	83.5	80.1	80.0	75.3
Per cent difference:				
U.S. - South	10.0	10.0	8.0	6.0
U.S. - "Core-South"	18.0	19.0	16.0	15.0

Source: U.S. Census of Population, 1960, General Social and Economic Characteristics, U.S. Summary, Bureau of the Census, 1962, Final Report PC(1)-IC.

APPENDIX 15   Per Cent of Four-Person Families[a] at Low Income Levels, by Color and Place of Residence, 1960

Income Class	All Families		Urban		Rural Non-farm		Rural Farm	
	Non-white	White	Non-white	White	Non-white	White	Non-white	White
	United States							
Below $2,000	15.7	3.5	9.5	1.8	35.7	4.9	69.4	19.2
Below $3,000	31.4	8.2	24.4	4.8	57.0	12.1	82.9	36.5
Below $4,000	48.5	16.5	42.3	11.2	72.2	24.2	88.8	52.1
	Outside the South							
Below $2,000	6.6	2.5	5.8	1.5	15.3	3.0	26.8	16.6
Below $3,000	15.8	6.2	14.6	3.9	29.0	8.2	43.7	34.0
Below $4,000	31.4	13.3	30.2	9.6	45.4	18.5	53.7	49.8

Source: U.S. Census Bureau, unpublished data.

a. Husband, wife, and two children under age 18; head of family male and employed.

Percentage Distribution of Occupied Housing Units by Number of Persons Per Room, for Total Population and Non-white Population at Low Income Levels, 1960

			Income[a]					
		Total	Below $2,000		$2,000-$2,999		$3,000-$3,999	
Persons	Total	Non-		Non-		Non-		Non-
Per Room	U.S.	white	All	white	All	white	All	white
All occupied housing units[b]	100	100	100	100	100	100	100	100
.50 or less	42	31	61	38	48	26	41	25
.51 to 1.00	47	41	29	35	37	40	44	42
1.01 or more	12	28	11	26	15	34	15	32

Source: U.S. Bureau of the Census, U.S. Census of Housing, 1960, Vol. II, Metropolitan Housing, Final Report, HC (2)-1; calculated from Tables A-3 and A-13.

a. 1959 income of primary families and individuals.

b. Figures may not total to 100 per cent because of rounding.

Percentage Distribution of Occupied Housing Units by Physical Condition, for Total Population and Non-white Population at Low Income Levels, 1960

Condition	Total U.S.	Total Non-white	Income[a]					
			Below $2,000		$2,000-$2,999		$3,000-$3,999	
			All	Non-white	All	Non-white	All	Non-white
All occupied housing units[b]	100	100	100	100	100	100	100	100
Substandard	23.8	55.9	48.9	74.9	38.4	61.8	30.9	51.0
Deteriorated	13.1	28.0	23.6	34.1	20.0	30.5	17.2	27.1
Dilapidated	4.3	16.8	11.2	26.0	7.1	17.7	5.0	12.8
Sound without plumbing	6.4	11.1	14.1	14.8	11.3	13.6	8.7	11.1
All sound	82.6	55.1	65.2	40.0	72.9	51.8	77.6	59.9
With plumbing	76.2	44.0	51.1	25.1	61.6	38.1	69.0	48.8
Without plumbing	6.4	11.1	14.1	14.8	11.3	13.6	8.7	11.1

Source: Same as Appendix 16.

a. 1959 income of primary families and individuals.

b. Component figures are those for "deteriorated," "dilapidated," and "all sound" as the "sound without plumbing" group is included in both "all sound" and "substandard."

Comparison of 1950 and 1960 Housing Census

It is, unfortunately, not possible to use the 1950 and 1960 Housing Censuses to make an exact evaluation of changes in the housing conditions of the low-income population. In 1950, housing was classified either as "dilapidated" or not; a third category, "deteriorating," was introduced in 1960. Technically, the standards for dilapidated were similar in 1950 and 1960 but it is not really possible to estimate how deteriorating housing in 1960 would have been classified in 1950. Numerous other definitional changes were made.

In Table A in this appendix all substandard housing facilities in 1960 and 1950 are compared. Here all 1950 housing reported as either "dilapidated" or not dilapidated but without complete plumbing is compared with all 1960 housing that was either sound but without complete plumbing, deteriorated and lacking some plumbing, or dilapidated. This comparison assumes that deteriorated housing with plumbing would have been classified as not dilapidated in 1950.

Note that Appendix 17 and Table A below use, for 1960, different criteria for the gross classification "substandard" housing which we have introduced; the estimate of substandard housing in 1960 is higher in Appendix 17 because all deteriorated housing is considered substandard, while Table A counts deteriorated housing as standard if it has complete plumbing facilities and as substandard if it does not.

Table A shows an improvement in the housing of the nation, and an improvement in the housing of the three lowest income groups; but the lowest income group shows the least proportionate improvement. Indeed, the poorest group, under $1,000 income in 1950 and under $2,000 in 1960, dropped from about three-fifths in substandard housing to about two-fifths. If the broader criteria of "substandard" used in Appendix 17 for 1960 housing had been applied to Table A, the improvement in housing conditions of the poor would be much smaller.

Housing for Non-whites

The same criteria can be used to compare changes in the conditions of housing for non-whites, between the 1950 and 1960 censuses. In 1950, about 73 per cent of housing units occupied by non-whites

TABLE   A   Per Cent of Housing Substandard, by Income Group,
             1950 and 1960

1950[a]	Total Population	Under $1,000	$1,000- $1,999	$2,000- $2,999
Dilapidated or Not Dilapidated and Lacks Some Plumbing	34.8	61.4	55.5	39.5

1960[a]	Total Population	Under $2,000	$2,000- $2,999	$3,000- $3,999
Dilapidated, Deteriorated, Lacks some plumbing, Sound lacks some plumbing	16.2	38.5	28.0	20.0

Sources: U.S. Census of Housing, 1950, Bureau of the Census, Vol. III, Farm
Housing Characteristics, Table 2, p. 4, and Non-Farm Housing Characteristics,
Vol. II, Part I, Table A-4, pp. 1-16; and Census of Housing, 1960, Vol. II, Met-
ropolitan Housing, Final Report, HC(2)-1. Calculated from Tables A-4 and A-13.
The 1950 census counted dwelling units and the 1960 census housing units, using
a slightly different definition.

  a. Income categories are the three lowest given for each census.

were substandard and in 1960, 44 per cent were substandard.[1] However, if the concept of substandard housing used in Appendix 17 is applied, there is less improvement in housing: from 73 per cent in 1950
to 56 per cent in 1960. Non-white housing has improved at a slower
rate than housing in general; at least part of the improvement can be
accounted for by Negro migration to urban areas during the decade.

  1. Bureau of the Census, Census of Housing, 1950, General Characteristics,
Part I, U.S. Summary, Vol. 1, Table 7, pp. 1-4. For analysis of some problems
in comparing the 1960 and 1950 Housing Censuses see Frank S. Kristof, "The In-
creased Utility of the 1960 Housing Census for Planning," pp. 40-47 and Lenore
R. Siegelman, "A Technical Note on Housing Census Comparability, 1950-1960,"
Journal of the American Institute of Planners, February 1963.

APPENDIX 19   Number and Percentage Distribution of Occupied Housing Units
by Physical Condition,
for Total and Non-white Population Inside and Outside Standard
Metropolitan Statistical Areas, 1960   (Number in Thousands)

Condition	U.S. Total Number[a]	U.S. Total Per Cent	U.S. Non-white Number	U.S. Non-white Per Cent	Inside SMSA's Total Number	Inside SMSA's Total Per Cent	Inside SMSA's Non-white Number	Inside SMSA's Non-white Per Cent	Outside SMSA's Total Number	Outside SMSA's Total Per Cent	Outside SMSA's Non-white Number	Outside SMSA's Non-white Per Cent
All occupied housing units[a]	53,024	100.0	5,144	100.0	34,000	100.0	3,487	100.0	19,024	100.0	1,658	100.0
Substandard[a]	12,592	23.8	2,878	55.9	5,732	16.9	1,505	43.2	6,859	36.0	1,372	82.7
Deteriorated	6,944	13.1	1,441	28.0	3,456	10.2	853	24.5	3,488	18.3	588	35.4
Dilapidated	2,267	4.3	863	16.8	980	2.9	388	11.1	1,289	6.8	475	28.6
Sound without plumbing	3,380	6.4	574	11.1	1,297	3.8	264	7.6	2,083	10.9	310	18.7
Sound with plumbing	40,432	76.2	2,266	44.0	28,268	83.1	1,981	56.8	12,165	63.9	285	17.1

Source: U.S. Bureau of the Census, U.S. Census of Housing, 1960, Vol. II, Metropolitan Housing, Final Report, HC(2)-1; calculated from Tables B-13 and C-14.

a. Figures may not add to total because of rounding.

Housing Conveniences of Recipients[a] of Old-Age Assistance, 1960

Convenience	Per Cent of Recipient Group		
	All Recipients	White	Non-white
Flush toilet			
For exclusive use of household	58.6	63.4	41.8
Shared with another household	6.8	6.8	6.8
No flush toilet	29.6	24.9	46.1
Unknown or other	5.0	4.9	5.5
Running water			
In building	74.2	78.9	57.5
Hot and cold	59.4	66.0	36.1
Cold only	12.0	10.3	17.9
Unknown	2.8	2.6	3.5
Outside building	4.2	2.7	9.5
No running water	19.7	16.5	30.9
Unknown	1.9	1.9	2.0
Mechanical refrigerator	82.5	87.0	67.0
Telephone	53.7	59.1	34.7
Electric lights	94.0	96.0	87.0

Source: U.S. Department of Health, Education, and Welfare, Characteristics and Financial Circumstances of Recipients of Old-Age Assistance, 1960, Part I, National Data, pp. 17, 18, 19.

a. Non-institutionalized recipients only.

182

Education and Income Levels in Public Housing vs. Surrounding Neighborhoods

	Median School Years Completed by Head of Household	Per Cent of 14-17 Year Olds in School	Mean Family Income
Public Housing Project A	9.0	78	$4,290
Adjoining tracts	8.1	74	4,811
Public Housing Project B	9.7	78	4,064
Adjoining tracts	8.7	69	4,774
Public Housing Project C	9.7	80	3,826
Adjoining tracts	7.7	76	4,117
Public Housing Project D	8.2	90	3,757
Adjoining tracts[a]	8.4	75	4,682

Source: Unpublished data of New York City Housing Authority, based on Bureau of Labor Statistics analysis of census data and relating to four public housing developments in 1960.

a. Adjoining tracts include some middle-income cooperatives in this area.

Incidence of Chronic Diseases,
by Income Level   (Age Adjusted)

	Below $2,000	$2,000–$4,000	$4,000–$6,000	Over $6,000
	I. Rate per 100,000 of Total Population			
All heart diseases	119.9	97.4	76.6	100.1
Coronary heart diseases and angina pectoris	27.0	20.9	28.9	23.6
Hypersensitive heart diseases	60.8	55.3	29.1	54.4
Hypersensitive without heart involvement	33.5	66.0	58.5	62.7
Syphilis	62.3	41.4	14.8	31.7
Diabetes mellitus	20.4	17.5	22.4	35.1
All arthritis	94.2	73.2	81.6	52.8
Diseases of female genital organs	172.3	223.7	160.6	120.4
	II. Rate as Per Cent of Rate in Lowest Income Class			
All heart diseases	100.0	81.2	63.8	83.4
Coronary heart diseases and angina pectoris	100.0	77.4	107.0	87.4
Hypersensitive heart diseases	100.0	90.9	47.8	39.4
Hypersensitive without heart involvement	100.0	197.0	174.6	187.1
Syphilis	100.0	66.5	23.7	50.9
Diabetes mellitus	100.0	85.7	109.8	172.0
All arthritis	100.0	77.7	86.6	56.05
Diseases of female genital organs	100.0	129.8	93.2	69.8

Source: U.S. National Health Survey, Health Statistics, Series B-7, B-8, B-10, Washington, 1960. Data apply to July 1958–June 1959.

APPENDIX 23

Per Cent of Families Carrying Health Insurance, by Family Income, 1959

	U.S. Total	Below $2,000	$2,000- $4,000	$4,000- $7,000	$7,000 and Over	Income Unknown
Hospital insurance	67.1	33.1	56.0	78.9	84.5	58.1
Surgical insurance	62.0	27.4	50.0	74.2	79.6	52.0
Medical insurance	19.3	8.9	14.1	21.9	27.7	17.9

Source: U.S. National Health Survey, Health Statistics, Series B-26, Tables 7, 8, and 9, Washington, 1960.

Per Cent of Population in the Labor Force, by Sex and Age Group, U.S. and Ten Representative Redevelopment Areas, 1960

Sex and Age Group	Nation	Average for 10 Redevelopment Areas	Per Cent Difference
Males:			
18–24	82.2	75.2	-7.0
25–44	97.6	94.3	-3.3
65 or over	32.3	24.2	-8.1
Females:			
18–24	45.5	42.5	-3.0
25–44	39.8	36.7	-3.1
65 or over	10.5	9.4	-1.1

Source: Statistical Profile of Redevelopment Areas, U.S. Bureau of the Census, Series SP, 1962.

Per Cent Not in the Labor Force, by Color, Sex, and Schooling, 1949–50 and 1959–60 (Noninstitutional Civilian Population)

Group	Per Cent Not in Labor Force Average 1949-50	Average 1959-60	Per Cent Increase or Decrease Over 1949-50
Total noninstitutional civilian population	41.8	41.7	- 0.2
Non-whites	36.6	38.1	+ 4.1
Males 65 or over	53.7	67.1	+24.9
Males 14-19	46.6	53.5	+14.8
Females 14-19	68.0	70.3	+ 3.4
With 8 years or less of schooling[a]	17.5	20.6[b]	+17.7

Sources: Current Population Reports, U.S. Bureau of the Census, 1948-58, Series P-50; Labor Force and Employment, U.S. Bureau of Labor Statistics, 1959-60, Special Labor Force Reports; Clarence D. Long, "An Overview of Postwar Labor Market Development," The Labor Market and Social Security, Proceedings of the Fourth Annual Social Security Conference, Upjohn Institute for Employment Research, Kalamazoo, Michigan, 1962.

a. Long, op. cit., Table 5, p. 23; figures for 1950 and 1959. Number not in labor force in 1950 adjusted to exclude institutional inmates from population and to exclude persons whose labor force participation was undercounted in the census of 1950, compared with the Current Population Survey.

b. 1959. Standardized for age according to the age composition of the population in 1950.

APPENDIX 26   Per Cent Unemployed and Duration of Unemployment, 1947-61

Year	Total Unemployed as Per Cent of Civilian Labor Force	Unemployed 15 Weeks or More			Unemployed 27 Weeks or More			Average Number of Weeks Unemployed
		As Per Cent of Labor Force	As Per Cent of Unemployed	3 Year Moving Average of Per Cent Unemployed	As Per Cent of Labor Force	As Per Cent of Unemployed	3 Year Moving Average of Per Cent Unemployed	
1947	3.9	0.7	16.9	--	0.3	7.0	--	9.8
1948	3.4	0.5	13.3	16.23	0.2	5.0	6.33	8.6
1949	5.5	1.1	18.5	18.37	0.4	7.0	7.57	10.0
1950	5.0	1.2	23.3	18.73	0.6	10.7	8.07	12.1
1951	3.0	0.5	14.4	16.57	0.2	6.5	7.17	9.7
1952	2.7	0.4	12.0	12.57	0.1	4.3	5.00	8.3
1953	2.5	0.3	11.3	15.33	0.1	4.2	5.80	8.1
1954	5.0	1.3	22.7	19.40	0.5	8.9	8.23	11.7
1955	4.0	1.1	24.2	21.97	0.5	11.6	9.57	13.2
1956	3.8	0.8	18.9	20.73	0.3	8.2	9.30	11.3
1957	4.3	0.8	19.1	23.00	0.4	8.1	10.17	10.4
1958	6.8	2.1	31.0	25.80	1.0	14.2	12.43	13.8
1959	5.5	1.5	27.3	27.53	0.8	15.0	13.57	14.5
1960	5.6	1.4	24.3	22.27[a]	0.6	11.5	14.40[a]	12.8
1961	6.7	1.0	15.2	--	1.1	16.7	--	15.5

Sources: Long-Term Unemployment in the United States, U.S. Bureau of Labor Statistics, 1961, Special Labor Force Report No. 17, Table A, p. A-2; 1947-56 data from Statistical Abstract of the United States, 1957, Table 243, p. 200; 1957-61 data from ibid, 1962, Table 280, p. 215.

a. Includes 1961.

Unemployment Rates by Sex, Age, Color, and Schooling, 1949–50, 1959–60, and Fourth Quarter 1962

Group	Average 1949-50	Average 1959-60	Fourth Quarter 1962	Per Cent Increase or Decrease Over 1949-50 1959-60	Per Cent Increase or Decrease Over 1949-50 Fourth Quarter 1962
Non-whites	8.8[a]	10.5	--	+19.3	--
Males 65 or over as per cent of 25-44 age group[b]	102.1	105.7	144.1	+ 3.5	+41.1
Males 14-19 as per cent of 25-44 age group[b]	287.0	342.9	361.8	+19.5	+26.0
Females 14-19 as per cent of 25-44 age group[b]	229.8	250.0	214.8	+ 8.8	- 6.5
Unskilled, weighted average[c]	6.7[a]	7.1	--	+ 6.0	--
With 8 years or less of schooling[d]	7.8[a]	9.3[e]	--	+19.2	--

Sources: Current Population Reports, U.S. Bureau of the Census, 1948-58, Series P-50; Labor Force and Employment, U.S. Bureau of Labor Statistics, 1959-60, Special Labor Force Reports; Clarence D. Long, "An Overview of Postwar Labor Market Developments," The Labor Market and Social Security, Proceedings of the Fourth Annual Social Security Conference, Upjohn Institute for Employment Research, Kalamazoo, Michigan, 1962.

a. Long, op. cit., Table 1, p. 19. Adjusted to include persons with job but not at work because of temporary layoff or waiting to start new job. Until 1957 the Census Bureau counted these persons as employed.

b. Calculated for each specific age group as per cent of the group 25-44 years old, differentiated by sex.

c. Long, op. cit., Table 2, p. 20.

d. Long, op. cit., Table 3, p. 21. Figures are for 1950 and 1959, not averages. All unemployment rates in 1950 adjusted upward for census undercount of labor force and unemployment, compared with the Current Population Survey.

e. Partially standardized according to the age composition of the civilian labor force in 1950.

Poverty-Unemployment Relationships, 1935–36, 1953, 1960

Income Level	Number Below Each Level (Millions)	Number (Thousands)	Unemployed Per Cent of Civilian Labor Force	As Per Cent of Number Below Each Income Level
1935–36		10,610	20.1	
"Comfort"	80.3			13.2
"Adequacy"	57.3			18.5
"Subsistence"	33.9			31.3
1953		1,900	2.3	
"Comfort"	61.1			3.1
"Adequacy"	35.7			5.3
"Subsistence"	22.7			8.4
1960		3,931	5.6	
"Comfort"	70.8			5.5
"Adequacy"	46.1			8.5
"Subsistence"	19.9			19.6

Sources: Number below each income level from Table A of Appendix 5. Employment and labor force data for 1935-36 from Historical Statistics of the United States, Colonial Times to 1957, U.S. Bureau of the Census, Series D1-12; for 1953 from Current Population Reports, U.S. Bureau of the Census, 1953, Series P-50; and for 1960 from Labor Force and Employment in 1960, U.S. Bureau of Labor Statistics, Special Labor Force Report No. 14.

Wages and Employment in Low-Wage Industries, 1960 (partial listing)

Industry	Average Wages Per Hour	Average Number of Production Workers and/or Non-supervisory Employees
Children's dresses, blouses, and shirts	$1.48	30,600
Apparel and accessories stores	1.47	582,000
Girls' and children's outerwear	1.46	67,500
Knit underwear	1.46	29,400
House furnishings	1.45	44,800
Cigars	1.44	26,000
Drug stores	1.43	347,500
Seamless hosiery	1.41	65,400
General merchandise stores	1.40	1,447,000
Women's and children's underwear	1.39	72,700
Poultry dressing and packing	1.36	57,600
Men's and boy's shirts and nightwear	1.32	105,500
Women's ready-to-wear stores	1.31	223,300
Work clothing	1.26	66,200
Laundries, cleaning and dyeing plants	1.24	389,200
Hotels, motels, and tourist courts	1.10	485,000
Limited-price variety stores	1.09	316,800

Source: "Employment and Earnings Statistics for the U.S.," Bulletin 1312, U.S. Bureau of Labor Statistics, 1961.

Estimated Number of Workers
Earning Below $1.50 Per Hour, 1960

	Number (Thousands)
Total below $1.50	8,109
Between $1.50 and $1.25	4,453
Below $1.25	3,656
In industries covered by federal minimum-wage legislation	5,159
Between $1.50 and $1.25	3,603
Below $1.25	1,556
In industries not covered by federal minimum-wage legislation	2,950
Between $1.50 and $1.25	850
Below $1.25	2,100

Sources: Based on Appendix 29 and on Hearings Before Subcommittee on Labor Standards, Committee on Education and Labor, House of Representatives, 86th Cong., 2nd sess., 1960.

APPENDIX 31

Calculation of the Public Anti-poverty Dollar

Appendices 32, 33, and 34 present the details of the New School poverty study staff's estimate of public anti-poverty expenditures in 1960. The method of calculation, described below, is essentially a two-way schema of costs related to poverty.

First are expenditures aimed at reducing the probability of being poor at some future time, listed in Appendix 32. The characteristics selected are those that were ascertained in this study to be closely related to poverty. Here our previous analysis is applied in terms of 1960 conditions. These expenditures are of two basic kinds: (1) costs of attempting to eliminate or reduce the incidence of the characteristic itself, such as the cost of medical research, which reduces the incidence of illness and thereby the incidence of poverty due to illness; (2) costs of attempting to reduce not the "weight" of the characteristic, but the "height of the probability of being poor if one has the characteristic"—it is not "old age" that is to be prevented but rather the probability of the "old being poor." Monies spent on disability are of both kinds: dollars are spent to prevent the occurrence of disability and also to provide alternative income opportunities for the disabled— that is, to reduce the probability that disability will lead to poverty by retraining for another job. Both types of expenditure are labeled "prevention."

To preventive costs must be added costs to alleviate poverty, listed in Appendix 33. Expenditures for the support of those officially declared poor are shown in the first column in this table, labeled "means test required." Again, in most cases these expenditures can be segregated by characteristic. The public costs of supporting persons not officially declared poor are included in the second column, "no means test required." These mainly involve veterans' benefits for which there are no income tests. For instance, a differentially determined monthly benefit is paid to service men who have become wholly or partly disabled as a direct result of military service. While the rationale is that their earning capacity has been impaired, they undergo no income test in order to receive benefits.

Obviously, many of the expenditures are for individuals with overlapping characteristics—one may be old, sick, and unemployed at the same time. Or, more correctly, one may be poor because he is unemployed, and he may be unemployed because he is sick, or because

he is old, or because he is old and uneducated. However, this problem in estimating the anti-poverty dollar is more conceptual than real,
since up to 1960 most of the anti-poverty programs in this country have
been established to deal with particular categories of people. For instance, we recognize under "old age" that the probability of being poor
when old actually reflects the probability of becoming a non-earner.
In fact, when the original Old Age and Survivors Insurance system was
set up, its purpose was to provide protection against loss of earned income in old age. In the same way, the probability of being poor because of sickness is nearly equivalent to the probability of not working
because of sickness. In other words, the "unemployment" category
covers only the case of being out of work for a reason not otherwise
accounted for in the structure of the tables.

The two-way presentation has the advantage of distinguishing, on
the intent side, between the recognition of the necessity of supporting
persons already poor and attempts to limit future poverty. However,
it does not give a proportionate division according to effect. The effect of some "supportive" programs is that they become "preventive,"
e. g., palliative programs in support of dependent children. (The two
subdivisions can be added, as in Table 3 in the text, with no danger of
double counting.)

Alternatives which were not used in our final calculations but
which were considered in the course of our analysis may be mentioned
briefly to illustrate other possible ways of arriving at the anti-poverty
dollar. It is obvious that expenditures may be ranked along a continuum reflecting different opinions about poverty and its causes. A four-
way classification could be constructed to subdivide expenditures into
those aimed at groups or characteristics which are: (1) "unmistakably" and "totally" poverty-linked (e. g., relief programs regulated by
means tests); (2) "unmistakably" and "partially" linked (e. g., unemployment compensation); (3) "less certainly" and "partially" linked
(e. g., expenditures on education and public health); and (4) "linked
only in a general socioeconomic way" (e. g., expenditures of the Council of Economic Advisors). Such a classification of spending, including costs to society as well as income flows to beneficiaries, is more
closely related to effect than to intent. Essentially, the categoriza-
tion is based on how low the incomes of the beneficiaries of the component of the anti-poverty dollar are, or on the probability of their
being poor; the program benefits under (1) would be paid out to persons already in abject poverty; those under (2) would go mainly to persons who are poor even with the benefits, but would be poorer without
them; those under (3) would benefit the entire population, but would
affect the poor to a greater extent; such expenditures, "less certainly"

and "partially" linked, also help reduce the probability of continued
poverty. Expenditures under (4) are expenditures meant to raise the
general level of economic growth and thus to prevent poverty by helping some poor persons, if fully effective.

Such a four-way division may be said to represent the analog of
the band of poverty to the extent that the band, besides being a reflection of existing policies, is also a reflection of the fact that "needs"
are perceived as relative. Classifying anti-poverty expenditures by
this method appears to have the disadvantage of being merely a way of
listing separately inclusions which may be debatable; a sophisticated
way of begging the question. In fact, however, by including in the various categories expenditures about which there can be no argument,
those about which there is some argument, and those about which there
is much argument, it provides useful policy guidance. A clear advantage of this approach, for instance, is that it isolates under classification (3) —"less certainly" and "partially" linked—those expenditures
whose direct relationship to poverty is often overlooked or "hidden."
Focusing the analysis on such expenditures is helpful, as it permits
establishment of priorities, along both a gradation of expenditures for
human needs and for economic reconstruction or growth.

The two-way approach that was decided upon reflects the New
School staff's belief that calculations that focus on intent—and particularly on "preventive" expenditures and their size—are of more use
for emerging policy.

Another approach that was rejected in calculating the anti-poverty
dollar involves distinguishing costs and benefits. Costs and benefits
may or may not be identical. In any classification of expenditures,
however, it is crucial to distinguish between them as a measure of the
efficiency of the anti-poverty effort. In Old Age, Survivors, and Disability Insurance, for example, in any one year, costs can perhaps
best be measured by OASDI taxes paid by workers and employers.
The total of these taxes will be a measure of society's effort, through
this particular program, to reduce the probability of being poor because of becoming an aged or disabled non-earner. In the same year
benefits are paid out to the aged and disabled who are entitled to them.
There are also administrative expenses. Together, benefits paid out
and administrative costs add up to total expenditures or outlays for the
year. However, the expenditures in a particular year are the result
of the effort, or outlays, in past years, not only by the recipient, but
by others. Were it necessary, Congress could also appropriate funds
for benefits from general tax revenues (as it did when, in 1961, extended unemployment insurance was established). Should this be the
case, the total cost, or effort, for the particular year would be the

sum of OASDI contributions (taxes) paid into the fund and those benefits paid out from general-revenue tax income.

Traditionally, those concerned with studying the condition of the
poor have measured society's efforts to cope with poverty primarily
by the money paid out to the poor. From this point of view and incor-
porating practice, a two-way income flow table, with two subdivisions,
might be devised, as follows: (1) benefits dependent upon a "means
test"; (1A) to those who remain poor, (1B) to those who are thus lifted
out of poverty (a very difficult measurement); and (2) benefits without
means test; (2A) to those who remain poor, (2B) to those who are not
poor. Theoretically, (2B) could be further broken down into benefits
which themselves have lifted recipients out of poverty (2Bi) and those
to persons who, by some other means, have been lifted out of low income (2Bii). The difficulties involved in this approach are obvious,
and any computation based on it would be subject to too much error to
be useful.

APPENDIX 32

Estimated Public Expenditures to <u>Prevent</u> Poverty, Fiscal Year 1960, by Program

(Expenditure Intended to Reduce the Association
Between Certain Individual Characteristics and Poverty)

Characteristic and Program	Expenditure (millions)	Notes
OLD AGE		
Old Age, Survivors, and Disability Insurance	$ 7,578.9	A portion of taxes for OASDI, based on ratio of age benefits to total benefits
Railroad Retirement Insurance	400.6	A portion of taxes for RR, based on ratio of benefits for aged and disabled 65 or over to total benefits
Civil Service Retirement	865.6	A portion of contributions to the system, based on ratio of benefits for aged and disabled 65 or over to total benefits
State & Local Government Employees' Retirement	1,714.3	A portion of contribution for retirement, based on established ratio of aged and disabled 65 or over to total
Veterans' Life Insurance	11.1	A portion of premiums-plus-government-appropriation, based on ratio of death benefits to total benefits
Subtotal	$10,570.5	
SICKNESS		
Medical Research	$ 460.0	Government funds for medical research, excluding training and education grants
Construction of Medical Facilities	525.7	Government funds for construction of hospital & other medical facilities, excluding military (Dept. of Defense)
School Health	101.0	Expenditures by educational agencies
Maternal and Child Health	139.4	Government funds for promotion of health of mothers and children. Includes crippled children program

197

Characteristic and Program	Expenditure (millions)	Notes
Temporary Disability Insurance	349.0	Contributions in 4 states with compulsory TDI coverage (Calif., N.J., N.Y., R.I.); calendar year
Railroad	36.9	A portion of railroad unemployment & sickness contributions, based on benefit ratio
School Lunch Program	368.9	Public funds & value of surplus food. Excludes cost of lunches included in Appendix 33 under "other"
Environmental Health: Federal	54.8	Public Health Service control programs
State and Local	348.0	Regulation and administration of sanitation, sewerage, water supply & other misc. public health services
Narcotics Control	4.3	Bureau of Narcotics of U.S. Treasury
Subtotal	$ 2,388.0	
PHYSICAL DISABILITY Accident Prevention	$ 7.4	U.S. Bureau of Labor Standards expenditures to promote industrial safety, plus U.S. Bureau of Mines, Health & Safety division expenditures
Workmen's Compensation	2,019.0	Employer contributions, state-fund premiums earned & federal benefits plus administrative expenditures. Includes est. cost for self-insurors
Vocational Rehabilitation: U.S. Office of Vocational Rehabilitation	93.7	Research & demonstration, medical & hospital care, prosthetics, training, & administration
Veterans Administration	6.5	Total expenditures for program, minus research and subsistence allowances
Disability Insurance	987.1	Taxes, state and federal
Railroad Disability Insurance	42.5	A portion of total contribution, to represent disabilities under age 65, based on benefits ratio

Characteristic and Program	Expenditure (millions)	Notes
Civil Service Disability	198.1	" " "
State & Local Government Employees' Disability	142.4	" " "
Veterans' Life Insurance	16.6	A portion of premiums plus govt. appropriations, based on ratio of disability income benefits to total benefits
Subtotal	$ 3,513.3	
ABSENCE OF BREADWINNER Old Age, Survivors, and Disability Insurance	$ 2,263.8	A portion of OASDI taxes, based on ratio of survivorship benefits to total benefits
Child Welfare	211.0	Total expenditures under federal & local program; includes payments for foster care
Railroad Survivorship	163.9	A portion of total contributions, based on ratio of survivorship benefits to total benefits
Civil Service Survivorship	213.2	" " "
State & Local Government Employees' Survivorship	343.4	" " "
Veterans' Life Insurance	526.4	A portion of premiums plus appropriations, based on ratio of survivorship benefits to total benefits
Subtotal	$ 3,721.7	
UNEMPLOYMENT Unemployment Insurance	$ 2,758.6	Contributions plus govt. appropriations, fed. & RR programs (RR based on portion of unemp. & sickness benefits going to unemployed)
U.S. Bureau of Employment Security	7.1	Fed. govt. link with local employment services
Subtotal	$ 2,765.7	
SUBSTANDARD & LOW-WAGE INDUSTRY U.S. Labor Department: Wage & Hour Division	$ 11.4	Administration & enforcement of the Fair Labor Standards Act & the Walsh-Healey Act

Characteristic and Program	Expenditure (millions)	Note
Bureau of Labor Standards	1.3	Technical service on workmen's comp., migratory & child labor, minimum wages, industrial relations: all BLS minus industrial safety
Compliance, Mexican Farm Labor	..9	Expenditures to enforce contract of payment of prevailing wage
Salary & Expenses, Mexican Farm Labor Program	1.3	Non-compliance aspects of program
Subtotal	$ 14.9	
LACK OF SKILL U.S. Labor Department: Bureau of Apprenticeship & Training	$ 3.9	Work with management & labor to formulate apprenticeship and on-the-job training, etc.
Vocational Education	233.1	Federal expenditures & state & local, for programs which meet standards under various vocational education acts
Subtotal	$ 242.0	
EDUCATION Elementary & Secondary Education: Current Expenditures	$11,476.6	
Construction	2,881.9	
Subtotal	$14,358.5	
NON-WHITE Commission on Civil Rights	$ .7	
Subtotal	$ .7	
Total	$37,575.3	

Note: As the Notes in the table indicate, where the nature of a given program is such as to benefit also the non-poor, e.g., OASDI, the amount entered refers only to a portion of total estimated public expenditures for that program. The amount was arrived at by estimating the proportion of beneficiaries of the program whose income in 1960 placed them within the poverty band.

Estimated Public Expenditures to <u>Alleviate</u> Poverty, Fiscal Year 1960, by Program

Charaeteristic and Program	Cost to Public in Benefits and Administrative Expenses (millions)		Notes
	Means Test Required	No Means Test Required	
OLD AGE			
Old Age Assistance	$2,014.7		
Public Housing for Elderly	18.4		
Medical Aid to Aged	122.8		Calendar year 1961 (first full year of operation)
Veterans' Service Pensions		$ 46.6	
Veterans' Domiciliary Care	14.2		
Subtotal	$2,170.1	$ 46.6	
SICKNESS			
Public Hospital Care	$2,017.7	$ 40.2	See Appendix 34. Includes mental hospitals
Veterans' Hospitals	454.1	412.9	See Appendix 34
Subtotal	$2,471.8	$ 453.1	
PHYSICAL DISABILITY			
Aid to Permanently & Totally Disabled	$ 302.9		
Aid to the Blind	100.2		
Aid to Families of Dependent Children	247.6		Families with incapacitated father
Veterans' Domiciliary Care	20.2		
Veterans' Pensions	883.6	$1,613.8	
Vocational Rehabilitation: U.S. Office of Vocational Rehabilitation	6.9		Subsistence allowances
Veterans' Administration		12.2	Subsistence allowances
Veterans' Paraplegic Welfare		4.8	Special autos & housing, net cost plus administrative expenses
Subtotal	$1,561.4	$1,630.8	
ABSENCE OF BREADWINNER			
Aid to Families of Dependent Children	$ 886.9		Families with absent father
Veterans' Death Compensation	473.4	$ 367.0	
Subtotal	$1,360.3	$ 367.0	

Characteristic and Program	Cost to Public in Benefits and Administrative Expenses (millions)		Notes
	Means Test Required	No Means Test Required	
OTHER			
General Assistance	$ 491.1		
Public Housing	158.3		Net subsidies (& administration) minus that portion for the elderly
Surplus Foods to Needy Families	59.4		
Free School Lunch	30.0		Estimated cost of lunches given free or at reduced price
Institutional Care	450.2		Homes for dependent persons (other than mental or Veterans Administration facilities) plus surplus foods to institutions
Subtotal	$1,189.0		
Total	$8,752.6	$2,497.5	

Public Payments to the Actually or Potentially Poor, Fiscal Year 1960, by Program (Millions)

Characteristic and Program	Means Test Required[a] Cash	In Kind[b]	No Means Test Required Cash	In Kind[b]	Notes
OLD AGE					
Old Age, Survivors, and Disability Insurance			$ 7,888.8		Benefits to aged[c] & their dependents
Railroad Retirement Insurance			630.3		Benefits to those aged 65 or over and their dependents
Civil Service Retirement			445.7		" " "
State & Local Government Employees' Retirement			620.0		" " "
Old Age Assistence	$1,614.3	$ 280.3			Net subsidies (& administration) for housing of those 65 or over
Public Housing for Elderly		18.4			
Medical Care to Aged		114.4			Calendar year 1961 (first full year of operation)
Veterans' Life Insurance			14.0		Matured endowment benefit payments
Veterans' Service Pensions			45.6		Pensions to veterans of Spanish-American, Indian, & Civil wars & dependents
Veterans' Domiciliary Care		14.2			Care of those 65 or over
	$1,614.3	$ 427.3	$ 9,644.4		
SICKNESS					
Temporary Disability Benefits			$ 293.9	$ 39.6	Benefits in 4 states with compulsory coverage; calendar year
Railroad Sickness Benefits			66.1		
Public Hospital Care		$2,017.7		40.2	State & local & D.C. hospitals, Indian hospital care & Canal Zone; includes mental hospitals
				(833.3)	Benefits to government employees & the military
Veterans' Hospitals		454.1		412.9	Allocated between means test & no means test on basis of number of patients undergoing income test for treatment
Subtotal		$2,471.8	$ 360.0	$ 492.7	
PHYSICAL DISABILITY					
Aid to Permanently & Totally Disabled	$ 225.1	$ 46.1			Cash & vendor payments
Aid to the Blind	84.7	7.6			" " "
Aid to Families of Dependent Children	210.6	13.0			Cash & vendor payments; estimated portion to those with disabled father in the house

203

Characteristic and Program	Means Test Required[a] Cash	In Kind[b]	No Means Test Required Cash	In Kind[b]	Notes
PHYSICAL DISABILITY (continued)					
Workmen's Compensation			775.0	420.0	Cash & hospital & medical benefits
Disability Insurance			578.3		Benefits from DI funds plus those from OASDI fund to disabled "children" 18 or over & their caretakers
Railroad Disability Insurance			$ 65.6		Benefits to disabled annuitants under age 65
Civil Service Disability			102.0		" " "
State & Local Government Employees' Disability			52.0		" " "
Vocational Rehabilitation:					
U.S. Office of Vocational Rehabilitation	$ 6.9			$ 79.7	Cash represents subsistence allowances; other represents goods & services, except research
Veterans Administration			12.2	6.5	" " "
Veterans' Paraplegic Benefits				4.0	Value of autos & grants for special homes, excl. admin. costs
Veterans' Domiciliary Care		$ 20.2			
Veterans' Pensions	$ 865.3		1,580.3		Disability pensions
Veterans' Insurance			25.1		Disability income benefits & premiums waived[d]
Subtotal	$1,392.6	$ 86.9	$3,190.5	$ 510.2	
ABSENCE OF BREADWINNER					
Old Age, Survivors, and Disability Insurance			$2,330.9		Monthly & lump-sum death benefits
Aid to Families of Dependent Children	$ 751.7	$ 46.4			ADC excl. portion to families where father incapacitated
Railroad Survivorship			214.2		Monthly & lump-sum death benefits
Civil Service Survivorship			109.9		" " "
State & Local Government Employees' Survivorship			124.0		" " "
Veterans' Death Compensation	463.6		359.4		" " "
Veterans' Life Insurance			434.6		Death benefits & optional income settlements
Workmen's Compensation Death			95.0		Death compensation
	$1,214.7	$ 46.4	$3,668.0		
UNEMPLOYMENT					
Unemployment Insurance			$2,698.3		State, federal & RR programs
Subtotal			$2,698.3		
OTHER					
General Assistance	$ 326.8	$ 99.2			Cash benefits & vendor payments
Public Housing		158.3			Net subsidies (& administration) minus that portion for the elderly
Surplus Foods to Needy Families		59.4			
Free School Lunch			$ 30.0		

Characteristic and Program	Means Test Required[a]		No Means Test Required		Notes
	Cash	In Kind[b]	Cash	In Kind[b]	
Institutional Care		450.2			Homes for neglected & dependent persons (other than mental, t.b., or Veterans Administration facilities) plus value of surplus foods to institutions
Veterans' Insurance Benefits, not elsewhere classified			317.9		Mostly dividends paid out to policy holders
Subtotal	$ 326.8	$ 767.1	$ 347.9		
Total	$4,548.4	$3,799.5	$19,909	$1,002.9	

a. Benefits contingent upon a "needs test."

b. Value of goods (plus administrative costs of certain programs) to approach as nearly as possible market value. Excludes free education.

c. As defined by Social Security Administration.

d. An undetermined portion represents insurance premiums waived.

Method of Calculating Per Cent of Disposable Personal Income Required to Raise the Poor to Three Budget Levels

To estimate the redistribution effort required to eliminate poverty, three basic steps were taken by the New School poverty study staff: (1) an estimate was made of the income required to lift up to each of our budget levels—"minimum subsistence," "minimum adequacy," and "minimum comfort"—those families and unattached individuals who were below these levels; (2) the income available for redistribution was calculated; and (3) the first figure was expressed as a percentage of the second. These estimates were made for a number of years. The budget levels were calculated by contemporary standards in current dollars (i. e., by a changing definition of poverty) and also by both 1960 and 1929 standards expressed in constant dollars. The procedure is illustrated in the accompanying table, which uses 1960 data and 1960 standards.

Line 1 of the table shows the dollar equivalent of each budget level, after needs have been adjusted to average family size by the method described in Appendix 5. The number of families and unattached individuals below each budget level (line 2) was derived from the family personal income series of the U.S. Department of Commerce, Office of Business Economics, in which series exact numbers are given to the nearest $1,000 income class. Adjustments for specific budget levels were made as follows: Assume that the income cut-off for families was $2,100 and the Office of Business Economics showed 1.7 million families below $2,000 and 1 million between $2,000 and $3,000; as $100 is one-tenth of the distance between $2,000 and $3,000, one-tenth of 1 million families would be estimated to fall between $2,000 and $2,100, and thus 1.8 million in all below $2,100. The same procedure was used for unattached individuals. In the highest and lowest income classes, straight-line interpolation was used except in cases where the majority of unattached individuals were in the Office of Business Economics income category below $1,000. In such cases a straight-line interpolation would be too risky and reference was made to the Brookings study of income, which provides a breakdown of units below $500 and between $500 and $1,000. If, for example, the cut-off for unattached individuals in a particular year was $472 and the Brookings study showed that approximately 40 per cent of unattached individuals with income below $1,000 received less than $500 in that year, the total number of unattached individuals below $1,000 according to the Office of Economics data was divided 40 to 60 and of the 40 per cent below $500 it was estimated that 94 per cent ($472/$500) fall below $472.

The estimates in line 3 of the amount of disposable personal income required to bring those below each budget level up to that level were obtained by multiplying the number of families and unattached individuals in line 2 by the dollar amounts in line 1. Line 4 shows what these units were estimated to be actually receiving in 1960. These estimates were made in a manner similar to that used in calculating the numbers below each budget level. If the cut-off level was $1,200, for example, the exact amount going to units below $1,000 would appear in the Office of Business Economics series and to it would be added 20 per cent of the amount received by the next $1,000 income interval ($200/$1,000).

Line 6 gives estimates of the amount of disposable personal income available for redistribution at each budget level, if an income at the "minimum comfort" level were guaranteed to those already above the level. The amount required to provide this guarantee was calculated at $163.5 billion, as follows. The number of families and unattached individuals whose income was above the "minimum comfort" level was calculated by subtracting from the 45,370,000 families and 10,690,000 unattached individuals in 1960 the numbers, shown in the table, with income below the "comfort" level. The remainders were then multiplied by the dollar values of the "minimum comfort" budget in line 1. Both the guarantee of $163.5 billion and the amount already going to those below each budget level (line 4 of the table) were subtracted from total disposable personal income ($351.8 billion in 1960) in order to obtain, for each budget level, the amount available for redistribution.

Line 7 expresses the additional amount required (line 5) as a percentage of the amount available for redistribution (line 6). It provides what might be called the redistribution percentages.

In calculating the redistribution percentages for 1929, the poverty study staff used 1929 standards from Appendix 2, Table A and the 1929 dollar values for disposable income.

TABLE A   Per Cent of Disposable Personal Income Required to Raise the Poor to Three Budget Levels, 1960

F: Families   I: Unattached Individuals

	"Minimum Subsistence"			"Minimum Adequacy"			"Minimum Comfort"		
	F	I	F+I	F	I	F+I	F	I	F+I
1. Dollar equivalent of budget level in 1960	$2,554	$1,277		$4,176	$2,088		$5,386	$2,693	
2. Number below budget level (thousands)	4,855	1,924		11,342	4,116		17,694	5,345	
3. Amount of disposable personal income required to bring those below each level up to that level (billions)	$12.4	$2.5	$14.9	$47.4	$8.6	$55.9	$95.3	$14.4	$109.7
4. Less amount received (billions)	8.4	1.9	10.3	30.5	4.5	35.0	60.1	7.6	67.8
5. Additional amount required (billions)	$ 4.0	$ .6	$ 4.6	$16.9	$4.0	$20.9	$35.2	$ 6.7	$ 41.9
6. Disposable personal income available for redistribution (billions)			$178.0			$153.3			$120.5
7. Additional amount required as per cent of amount available for redistribution			2.6%			13.6%			34.8%